"Fudge"

The Downs and Ups of a Biracial, Half-Irish British War Baby

a memoir
Pauline Nevins

"My memory isn't perfect, but I haven't deliberately invented situations or facts. I have rearranged timelines, and I have changed some names to protect the privacy of those individuals. I realize that others who experienced the same situations that I did, may have perceived or remembered events differently—that's the nature of memory."

Pauline Nevins

COPYRIGHTS:

Memoir published and copyrighted in 2015 and 2019 by author, Pauline Nevins. First printed in the United States of America in 2015.

ALL RIGHTS RESERVED – This memoir has all rights reserved, is protected by copyright, and may not be reproduced, transmitted, stored, or used in any form or by any means graphic, electronic, or mechanical, including but not limited to photocopying, recording, scanning, digitizing, taping, Web distribution, information networks, or information storage and retrieval systems without the prior written permission of the author.

pauline@nevins.org

Cover design by Aaron Nevins
www.aaronnevins.com

Dedicated to my children,

Dean, Tina and Aaron

Unlike my mother's life—

your mother's life is an open book.

*"Yesterday is History,
Tomorrow a Mystery,
Today is a Gift,
That's why it's called the Present"*

Author Unknown

Illustrations – Attributions

1.1 Croyland Road Junior School Photograph,   2
Wellingborough, Northamptonshire 1952
Courtesy of Bill Cripps and Jean Cripps

1.2 Inside of a British Phone Box circa 1950   48
Courtesy of Pat Cryer 'Join me in the 1900's'
www.1900s.org.uk

2.1 Woolworth's Shop, Market Street   58
Wellingborough, Northamptonshire circa 1977
Courtesy of Andrew Bettts, Wellingborough

2.2 The Lyric Cinema   67
Wellingborough, Northamptonshire
Courtesy of cinematreasures.org

2.3 John Lea Secondary Modern School   100
Wellingborough, Northamptonshire
Courtesy of Trevor Jones

3.1 Teddy Boys – circa 1950s   107
Courtesy of Ryan Chang
www.volibroklyn.com

3.2 Cliff Richard – Britain's answer to Elvis   135
Courtesy of Allan Warren/Wikipedia

3.3 Doris – Wellingborough Parade 1959   138
Courtesy of Andy Davis via Andrew John Law
Facebook page: Wellingborough Now & Then

3.4 BMW 3-Wheel Bubble Car   142
   Courtesy of Oldfarm/English Wikipedia

4.1 Cover of DWR Newsletter 1979   206
   *Courtesy of the California Department
   of Water Resources*

5.1 The Hind Hotel Wellingborough   246
   *Courtesy of Ian Hamilton, General Manager of the
   Hind Hotel*

5.2 William Chapman   286
   Courtesy of Dawn Holloway

CONTENTS

Acknowledgements	xi
MIRROR MIRROR	3
BETTE AND HARRY	8
84 MANNOCK	18
WHAT'S A MULATTO?	30
AUNTIE MARGARET	34
PRESSS BUTTON "A"	39
SPUD BASHING AND OTHER MONEY MAKERS	51
CONKERS ANYONE?	59
HE FORGOT TO PAINT THEM	68
TOP OF THE MORNIN'	73
YOU SHOW ME YOURS	76
ELEVEN PLUS	81
STITCH IN TIME	89
MATERIAL GIRL	103
THE FANCY MAN	108
A BIRD IN THE HAND	120
ONE FRIDAY NIGHT	125
THE CRICKET QUEEN	136
MR. RIGHT	139
FRANK THE YANK	145
WILBY LIDO	159
LOVING VS VIRGINIA	165
THE OLIVE TWIG	173
ONE ENCHANTED EVENING	177
FRIENDS AND FAMILY	186
STICKS AND STONES	194
HELLO AND GOODBYE	208
DO NOT BEND	215

I WANDER LONELY	219
DORIS AND SID	225
"GOODBYE LOVE, NO ONE'S LEAVING"	229
GONE FOR GOOD	247
A TANGLED WEB	256
A GOOD BUZZ	265
CONCLUSION	277
THE REST OF THE STORY-Summer 2019	287
ABOUT THE AUTHOR	303
ALSO BY THE AUTHOR	304

Acknowledgements

To my husband, Jim, for your love and your support.

To my daughter, Tina, for your unwavering encouragement in everything I've ever attempted.

To my sons, Dean and Aaron—Dean for your helpful input, and Aaron for sharing your artistic talents.

To my brother, Kevan, for remembering events I'd forgotten and for correcting some I'd remembered.

To members of the Coffee, Tea and Saki Writers' Group: Richard Fay, Bill and Barbara Neville, Bill and Donna Simmons, and Miyoko Zwarich, for your acceptance, your encouragement, and most of all, for your friendship.

To editors Sue Clark, Alan Rinzler, Suzanne Sherman, and Linda Joy Myer, for your early-stages feedback, and in particular, to Donna Meares for your professional advice and wise counsel during final reviews.

To Wellingborough author, Sue Chambers, who inspired me with her delightful book: "The Other Half of the Crescent."

PART ONE
Who am I?

Wellingborough 1952

MIRROR MIRROR

"You, the colored girl in the second row, please move over a little."

I was sitting as still as I could be, waiting with all the other little eight-year-olds to have our school photograph taken outside Croyland Road Junior School in Wellingborough—a small town in England's East Midlands.

The photographer pointed at me.

"Yes, you, the colored girl. Move a bit to your left, please."

Colored girl?

I turned around to see who he was talking to. The other kids giggled.

Oh, yes, he meant me.

It may have been I simply had a bad memory. What else could explain how I kept forgetting I looked different from everyone else in my family, and from most of the people around me? Even my nickname, "Fudge," wasn't a reminder.

Not long after, I was alone at home. It was a hot summer day. Mother had left me the money to pay the rent. I was sitting at the kitchen table watching the flies stick to the flypaper tacked to the ceiling when the rent man knocked at the back door. I handed him the rent money and he made a notation in our rent book.

"It ent half hot ent it," he said in his strong.

Wellingborough accent as he handed back the book. Then he gave me a pleasant smile. "Oh, but you're prob'bly used to this weather where you come from."

I managed a smile and snatched back the rent book. *Well, where would that be? I was born in England just like you.*

The rent man wasn't being unkind. My skin was brown and my hair was black and frizzy—not exactly a typical English look. It was also 1952, and there were few non-whites in our small country town.

I've often wondered if I would have been more conscious of looking different from the majority of those around me, if, as the rent man assumed, I'd been the child of Jamaican or West Indian immigrants. Their dark faces would have been my reflection, and my reminder. As it was, everyone in my family was white—my mother, stepfather, seven brothers and sisters, an aunt, uncles and cousins. They were not only white—they were Irish.

One of my older sisters said maybe I was a "throwback." It didn't sound like a compliment.

"Why does your Pauline have brown skin?" a curious friend of my brother's once asked. My brother looked at him as if he were stupid.

"Because she fell in a bucket of brown paint," was his reply.

The truth was less dramatic. My mother was white, and my biological father was some mysterious, unknown, black man.

My situation was particularly puzzling because I was Bette Behan's fourth child. My mother, and stepfather, Harry Behan—whom we called "Dad" to his face, and "the Old Man" behind his back—had three children together before I came along, all one year apart. Sheila was the eldest, born in 1940, then Terry, and Doris. I was born in

"Fudge"

1944. Mother and Harry would go on to have four more children after me: Kevan, Eileen, Billy, and Delluna—who we all called Delly.

Since I was a middle child, it was difficult to conjure up Mother being married to my father before she met Harry. I overheard my mother telling a friend she wasn't sure what color I was going to be before I was born. They both laughed. I didn't get the joke.

In keeping with Mother's secretive nature, she never told me anything about my father, or mentioned the Old Man's reaction to my birth. Harry must have been around at the time because Eire, the Republic of Ireland, where he and my mother were born, was neutral during World War II, and the Old Man wouldn't have been conscripted into the army.

Decades later I learned from reading Kerry McDermott's "Daily Mail Online," there were thousands of Irishmen who did fight. They left the Irish Army and joined the British in the fight against the Nazis. They were branded deserters and court martialed when they returned to Ireland. Seven decades after the war, the Irish government pardoned these brave men. For many the pardon came too late.

The one thing Mother did tell me was that I was born with double pneumonia, and she'd slept by the open coal fire with me beside her.

"I put you in a dresser drawer. It was smaller than a cot, and I could keep you warmer," she'd said. "I tore off the corner of a piece of newspaper and placed it over your mouth so I could look from my bed and see it rise and fall with your breath."

I must have smiled hearing the story—this sign my mother cared, and wanted to keep me. I was afraid to ask my mother for any details about my father. I assumed her silence meant she was ashamed. What little I learned came from overhearing snippets of conversation between my mother and female neighbors.

One afternoon I dawdled passed Mother and Mrs. Anderson as they gossiped at the kitchen table, each wearing a wrap-around pinafore, their hair wound in pink plastic curlers, as they took deep drags of Woodbine cigarettes, and swigged Brooke Bond tea. Mother and her friend were reminiscing about the war years. Judging by their laughter, a good time was had by all.

"Bette, remember what they used to say about the Yanks?" my mother's friend said, flicking ash in a saucer. "They're overpaid, they're oversexed, and they're over here." They both coughed and laughed at the same time, almost choking on their cigarette smoke.

"There was another one too. They said there was a new brand of women's knickers—one yank and they're off." More laughter.

And it was from snippets like these, and a lack of any other possibility, I concluded my father was an American soldier.

What did my father look like? Where in America was he born? How did he and my mother meet? Most of all, I wondered if he knew, or cared, he'd left behind a baby with dark skin and frizzy hair, physical attributes wasted on an island with perpetual cloud cover.

Mother, Age 50
Finedon, Northamptonshire 1967

My favorite photograph

BETTE AND HARRY

If there was such a thing as looking typically Irish, then my mother would've fit the description. Her hair was black, her face long and thin and her nose narrow. A look of pain, just leaving, or coming, seemed to lurk in her light gray eyes. Her translucent white skin exposed the blue veins in her arms and hands, and the varicose veins in her thin legs. She was neither short nor tall, with "not much meat on her bones"—an expression Mother was fond of using. One afternoon, someone was taking a rare photograph of a group of us in the backyard. Mother took off her pinafore, and then held up her hand to halt the picture. She went in the house and came out with a couple of socks. Laughing, she put her hand down the front of her dress and stuck a sock inside each cup of her bra to give herself some shape.

Mother's uniform was a flowered wrap-around pinafore, although she never splurged on any clothes worth protecting. She'd cut her hair when it reached the bottom of her ears, then wrapped it up in a scarf, turban-style. Inside the house she wore rubber-soled woolen slippers with a hole cut on each side to allow the swollen corns on her little toes to poke through. There were times when Mother was too tired to remove her brown nylon stockings, and they'd end their journey around her ankles.

My mother was born Elizabeth Mary Halligan, in Castlebar, County Mayo, Ireland, in 1917, and crossed the Irish Sea to London when she was 17 years old. She worked for a Jewish family in London when she first came over—helped by an organization which placed young Irish women as domestic workers in wealthy homes.

Mother's past was a mystery to all of us kids, but once in a while she would open up. As I walked into the kitchen one afternoon after school, Mother passed me as she pulled on her woolen cardigan over her pinafore.

"Where are you going?" I asked, surprised. Mother rarely left the house.

"I'm going next door to help Eunice until the midwife gets there."

"What's a midwife?" I asked. She ignored my question and hurried out the back door.

Later in the evening as I worked on my homework at the kitchen table, Mother came into the room and lit the gas under the kettle on the stove to boil water for her night-time cup of tea. She sat down in the chair beside me, crossing one thin bare leg over the other. The Old Man was out drinking and the rest of the kids were in bed.

"My mother was a midwife," she said after taking a long drag on her cigarette. I almost dropped my pencil. When my mother spoke to me, it was to tell me what to do, and where to go. Now here I was, in a house which was quiet for a change, and my mother was talking to me, telling me something about her mother.

"She would drive a pony and trap to the farms to deliver the babies. The families would pay her with live chickens."

I looked at my mother as she stared off into space. I didn't say a word. I imagined her as a young girl, maybe eight-years-old, like me, sitting side-by-side with her mother in the trap, rumbling over bumpy roads. There would be fields of "fresh and green" as far as they could see—just like in the Irish ballad, "I'll take you home again Kathleen"—a song my mother sang.

"Time to go to bed," she said.

She never told me anything else about my grandmother. She never mentioned her father.

The f-word was standard language around our house. Mother used the word matter-of-factly. I didn't swear. I didn't even use slang. My aberrant behavior often elicited a, "Who do you think you are—Lady Muck?" from my sister Doris—a slang user, and another avid swearer. Doris would toss back her head when she fired these missives, and strands of her stringy brown hair would slide out from beneath her headscarf—an accessory she rarely removed, even inside the house.

"You're not intelligent enough to use the proper words—that's why you swear," I'd tell Doris with a sniff.

"Up yours," was her usual response.

I'd also try to rein in my mother.

"My friends are coming over," I'd tell her. "Please don't swear."

"Who the f--k, do you think they are?" my mother would say. Then she'd knock off the swearing, and acts like a perfect lady. This transformation by my mother occurred in front of others too.

Kevan, a younger brother, was in bed with the mumps one winter looking more cherubic than usual with his swollen cheeks. Kevan was a good-natured, cheerful, good-looking kid with a mop of blond curls. He was the only child in the family who managed to get along with everyone. As he lay in bed, two of my brothers and I were squabbling over a Beano comic book. Mother pulled aside the curtain at the bay window to see who knocked at the front door. She whipped around and faced us.

"Behave or I'll cut the f--king jib of ye," she threatened.

Mother opened the front door to our family doctor—one visitor we'd never have seen if it weren't for the free medical care of the National Health Service.

Even with his trilby removed, Dr. Carpenter had to stoop to enter the front door.

"Hello, Doctor. Please come in," Mother said in her best British accent, stunning the three of us kids into silence. You'd have thought he was royalty. She almost curtsied.

Mother had no such respect for the actual British Royal Family. She took particular delight in casting dispersions on their physical appearance—focusing on the length of their noses, and their unsuitable attire. I walked into the living room one afternoon to find her staring at the flickering black and white television in the corner.

"She looks like a gypo," my mother said with disgust—using the abbreviated derogatory word for a Romani. She couldn't believe the Queen of England would appear at a horse race dressed in a raincoat and headscarf, looking decidedly unqueenly.

I looked at my mother. There she was, mocking the Queen, with one eye on the horse race, the other squeezed tight against the stream of smoke from the cigarette clasped between her lips. She had one bare foot propped on a chair while she took a break from paring the dead skin off the corn on her little toe with the Old Man's Gillette razor blade.

Years of going shoeless in the Irish fields, and then having to cram those feet into the sensible shoes of an immigrant domestic, played havoc with Mother's feet. There would be many evenings when I would come in from playing in the street to find Mother trying to soothe her aching "plates." A chipped white enamel bowl would be steaming by the blazing coal fire. Mother sat in a straight-back wooden chair, her pinafore and dress pulled up to her knees exposing her thin, blue-veined legs. "Ouch," she'd say as she attempted to lower her sore feet into the scorching water sprinkled with Epsom salts.

Mother never embraced England as her home, despite living in the country for decades. She refused to forget, or forgive, the oppression of the Irish by the English. My Catholic mother wasn't too fond of the Irish Protestants either, who mostly lived in the six northern Irish counties belonging to Great Britain.

"They're Orangemen," she'd say disgustedly whenever anything about the Northern Irish came over the wireless.

I'd have to wait for a history lesson to find out that the "Orangemen," she referred to were supporters of William of Orange, the Protestant King of England, who'd deposed the Catholic King James II, then defeated him in the Irish Battle of the Boyne. According to some records, James abandoned his Irish supporters and returned to France where he'd been living in exile. His hasty retreat earned him the nickname Seamus a'chaca, which translates to "James the Shit." The Battle of the Boyne was fought in the 17th century, confirming Mother's own admission she had a memory like an elephant.

The Old Man was 12 years older than Mother—which accounted for the "Old Man" nickname she gave him. Others called him Harry, although he was born Henry Behan, in County Kildare in 1905. He appeared to me to be a big man, although he wasn't heavy, or tall. He never looked quite clean, even after he washed his face in the kitchen sink. His pores were filled with the soot from the railway yard on Midland Road where he worked as a laborer. The navy-blue bib overalls, issued by the British Railway, looked as if he never took them off. The color of his heavy lace-up leather boots was disguised under layers of grime. His hair was brown, and thinning. The Old Man never left the house without his worn, stained flat cap, which he hung on a nail hammered into the living room wall.

"He's a street angel and a house devil," my mother said one day as she looked at the Old Man through the white net curtains in the bay window. He was talking and laughing with a neighbor outside the front gate, exposing his two nicotine-stained front teeth.

If it was too cold outside, the Old Man wouldn't hesitate to stay home from work. He couldn't pass a pub without stopping in, and on many a payday, would squander his wages before he made it home.

Although I didn't see the Old Man hit my mother, there were evenings I'd hear their shouts, the swearing, and the banging and crashing from downstairs. Those nights I'd pull the bed covers over my ears to block out Mother's strangled cries as she'd scream, "You drunken bastard."

Judging from some of the conversations I overheard, the Old Man's drinking had always been a problem.

Mother's voice drifted through the tiny open window high up on the outside wall of the lavatory as I sat on the toilet, delaying the time when I'd have to wipe my bum with a rough piece of the *News of the World*. She was talking to Mrs. Cook over the privet hedge separating our backyards. Mrs. Cook, whose first name was Kitty—a name I never used because you were taught to call all adults Mr. or Mrs.—was a plump, gray-haired, soft-spoken woman. She, and her husband, Mr. Cook,—Arthur, if you were an adult—was a quiet couple. I can only imagine what it was like for them living next to our chaotic family.

"The Old Man came home so blind drunk one night," I heard my mother say. "He pulled out each dresser drawer and pissed in it. Soaked all the clothes." Mother's voice got louder at the end. She sounded angrier about the ruined clothes than about the Old Man being drunk. My ears pricked up higher when I heard Mother mention my brother Terry's name.

"Terry had his days and nights mixed up when he was a baby."

I was hoping I'd hear the rest of the story before someone banged on the lavatory door and said, "Hurry up,"—a regular occurrence with seven other kids sharing the toilet.

"I'd put him in the pram and walk up and down the street in the middle of the night trying to rock him to sleep," my mother continued. "The Old Man threatened to kill us both if I couldn't quiet him down."

Mother was talking about when Terry was a baby and they lived in Rushden. Was that why the Old Man picked on Terry so much?

I thought about what happened last Saturday.

The rain was coming down in buckets, and the wind blew so hard it rattled the window panes. Several of us kids were shoving each other against the black fire guard, fighting for a space to keep warm. My older brother, Terry, was sitting in Mother's easy chair by the bay window reading the "Dandy" comic. His grey wool knee socks had slid down to his ankles. The two bony knees exposed below his short trousers, looked like they could use a good scrub. Terry, like my other two brothers, was nice enough looking, but he lacked the sunny disposition of Kevan, or the endearing mischievousness of our youngest brother, Billy. That afternoon, Mother puttered about in the kitchen. The Old Man was repairing one of the top steps of the staircase leading to the three upstairs bedrooms. We all froze when we heard the Old Man's voice.

"Terry, bring me a spanner," he shouted.

Terry dropped his comic and rushed up the stairs with a tool.

"You bastard," we heard the Old Man roar.

Then we heard the slap. Terry cried out as he went crashing backwards down the stairs landing in a heap at the bottom. He slowly picked himself up, holding his head as he came into the living room. Mother rushed towards Terry screaming, "Jesus Christ Almighty."

Terry had handed the Old Man the wrong tool.

Depending on his mood, the Old Man could dole out punishment indiscriminately. When one kid did something wrong, we'd all get it. He would stand up, and slowly take off the brown leather belt with the brass buckle he wore on the outside of his overalls. He'd line us up, open the door to the hallway, and give each of us a whack with the belt as we ran for the stairs. I'd start screaming long before I felt the sting of the belt. Even though I wasn't his kid, the Old Man didn't whack me any harder, or any more often, than the rest of the kids.

Animals were not immune from the Old Man's brutality. Just before teatime one Sunday afternoon, the Old Man sat in the living room in his usual position—legs propped up on the fire guard, his full weight tilted back on two legs of the brown wooden chair, a hand-rolled cigarette clasped between his lips.

Mother busied herself in the kitchen carrying food from the pantry to the kitchen table. She'd placed a plate with a ham hock next to the loaf of white bread, and, then turned to go back into the pantry. While her back was turned, and before I, or any of the other kids could stop it, the neighbor's cat leapt on the table, snatched the ham hock and knocked it to the floor. The Old Man heard the commotion and strode into the kitchen, cornered the cat, took off his cap, and used it to practically beat the poor animal to death. We all screamed for him to stop—cries he ignored. The Old Man booted the poor animal out the back door into the yard, where it dragged itself into the safety of the neighbor's hedge.

The Old Man was uncouth as well as cruel. Impatient to drink his hot tea, he'd speed up the cooling by pouring it into the saucer, and then slurped it up. Bad as this was, it paled in comparison to his nightly ritual of blowing the railroad soot out of one nostril into the open coal fire. He'd miss his target and the snot would sizzle on the front grate.

The early morning dew would still be on the grass when the Old Man occasionally marched a group of us across the street to Croyland Park. I skipped along with the rest of the kids, happy to be going somewhere with the Old Man. Inside the park we followed him across the field and gathered around the circle of fungi in the grass where he'd pointed. The Old Man told us it was a fairy circle, which was how you tell mushrooms from poisonous toadstools—mushrooms grew in a circle. I doubt this was the most reliable way to tell the difference between the two, but nobody died.

We'd return home with the picked mushrooms and

Mother would peel off a little of the outer skin, remove the stems, put a bit of butter, and a pinch of salt, in the upturned caps, and simmer them on the black iron grate in front of the coal fire. This was the same grate where the Old Man blew his nose.

84 MANNOCK

None of us kids knew how Mother and the Old Man met. They didn't grow up in the same town. Mother was born in Castlebar, County Mayo, in the West of Ireland. The Old Man was born in Kildare, further south and to the east. There were no photographs to offer hints of an earlier life, or to tell us there were happier times. We could only guess when, and how, they ended up in Wellingborough, the East Midland town where all of us kids grew up.

"Your mum and dad have Irish accents," my friends would tell me—but I couldn't hear it. I knew they used phrases other parents didn't, such as, "Will ye whisht," for "Will you be quiet," and Mother called us "eejits," or "amadans" instead of idiots. Both of them would call my brothers a "fairy man" if they got into mischief. They used threats of violence constantly: "I'll swing for ye," either of them might say as they made a grab for you. "I'll cut the jib of ye," was another. "Gossoons," meaning "young boys," was about the only Irish word I heard not linked to a threat, a curse, or an insult.

As far as I knew, Mother and the Old Man returned to Ireland only once. They took some of my brothers and sisters with them. Sheila, Kevan, and I were left at home. I never learned which town, or which relatives, they visited. Our sister, Doris, told us the house they stayed in "didn't half stink." Apparently, the cows and other farm animals slept inside with the family. I never understood why Mother and the Old Man didn't take Kevan to Ireland with them. He wouldn't have been an embarrassment to them like Sheila and I would've been—Sheila with her one arm, and me with my brown skin and frizzy black hair.

No mention was ever made as to why Sheila was born with one arm—her right arm ended just below the elbow. This mystery, just like my appearance, led to all kinds of speculation. A friend, who'd met Sheila when she was adult, asked me if Mother had taken the anti-morning sickness drug, Thalidomide, which caused thousands of birth defects. I knew Mother hadn't taken anything because Sheila was born years before the drug was on the market.

I overhead Mother telling a neighbor that Sheila was born under the bed during one of Germany's deadly bombing raids when they were targeting London civilians. More than 23,000 British people were killed during July through December 1940. Sheila was born October 25, 1940.

Another time I heard the Old Man, drunk, had knocked Mother down the stairs when she was pregnant with Sheila. The bombings, or mother's fall, seemed about as plausible a cause for Sheila's missing arm, as tumbling into the brown paint bucket was to my skin color.

Terry was born a year after Sheila, in Rushden, a country town about 70 miles north of London. Millions of women and children were evacuated from London to the countryside in 1940 to protect them from the German bombing raids. I'd guessed this was when Mother and Sheila came to live in Rushden. My guess was confirmed one afternoon.

I'd run all the way home from school, anxious to get in out of the rain and thunder. As I opened the back door into the kitchen and scurried through the living room to hang up my dripping coat in the hallway, I was surprised to find that my mother was in neither room. On my way back into the kitchen to grab some food before the rest of the kids came home, I saw a thin line of grey smoke drifting from the direction of the gas cupboard—the small room under the stairs where the gas meter was located. There I found Mother, sitting in a chair, in the dark, smoking a cigarette. Mother set aside her usual, "It's none of your business," when I asked her what she was doing.

"When it thunders this bad," she said, waving her cigarette, oblivious to the fact she was sitting in a gas cupboard, "it brings back terrible memories of the London bombings. I wouldn't go to the air raid shelters. People got buried alive in those things. I took my chances in the street."

Mother wasn't exaggerating. She lived in London during the time the Germans rained bombs down on the city for 57 nights in a row, killing tens of thousands. These devastating bombardments were called "The Blitz," short for Blitzkrieg—German for "Lightning War."

No wonder Mother hid in the cupboard and smoked.

* * *

The Old Man and Mother moved from Rushden to nearby Wellingborough to work at RAF Chelveston, the British air base being turned over to the American Eighth Air force. I have no idea how Mother managed to go to work when she was popping out babies at the rate of one a year. Doris, their third child, was the first to be born in

Wellingborough, a year after Terry's birth in Rushden. I was born 15 months after Doris. It was obvious to anyone who could see that the Old Man was not my father, but I never heard a word about his reacting violently to my mother's pregnancy, or telling her to get rid of me. Mother and the Old Man had four more children together after me, which would indicate my arrival had no immediate effect on at least one aspect of their relationship.

For years I thought I was born in Gold Street in Wellingborough. I liked the idea of being born on a street named after a precious metal. I was an adult the first time I saw my long-form birth certificate. It was printed on rose-colored parchment paper. Under the column, "When and Where Born," was the address. I thought I wasn't seeing straight. Instead of the lovely-sounding Gold Street, it read "Brooke Street West," a creepy, dark street everyone dashed passed when walking into town. I did another double take when under "Name and Surname of Father" was "Harry Behan." I'm not sure what name I expected to see, but it was a shock to see the Old Man's name in print—accepting me as his own. It might have had something to do with qualifying for an extra few shillings of family allowance.

My brother, Kevan, was born a year after me, and was the youngest of the five kids, all under the age of eight, who eventually moved with Mother and the Old Man from Brooke Street West to a new house in Mannock Road. I was four-years-old at the time. The last three kids, Eileen, Billy, and Delly, would be born a year apart in the new house, and bring the total number of children to eight.

Our house on Mannock Road looked like millions of others that the local governments, called Councils, built all over Britain to replace homes destroyed by German bombs, and to give returning soldiers somewhere to live.

I never felt stigmatized living in a subsidized council house—Wellingborough was full of them. These houses were in such demand waiting lists were established. Sections of our town included homes known as "private" houses—owned by their occupants. I'd dawdle by them, admiring the large gardens and the colorful stained-glass in the front door panels and the bay windows. A front door might open as I passed by and give me a glimpse of plush carpets and spacious rooms.

All the council houses had small front yards, and larger backyards. If you lived on a corner, as we did, you had an additional strip of land on one side.

When a visitor clicked open the latch on our wooden green front gate they were greeted by Mother's favorite orange and red wallflowers neatly framing the patch of grass on the right side of the garden path. On the left were rows of cabbages, potatoes and brussel sprouts, planted by the Old Man.

Two rusty bikes leaned against the sheet of corrugated metal propped against the hedge outside the back door. One bike was the Old Man's, and the other was shared by the rest of us kids. Cars were rare in our neighborhood. Everyone biked, rode the bus, or walked to wherever they needed to go. Mother's mangle, a contraption for squeezing water out of washing, and a metal tub, were parked next to the bikes. A couple of orange-feathered bantam hens, and a red-headed rooster Mother named Ringo, pecked around in the chicken hutch that occupied the rest of the space on that side of the yard. A large, black, open-topped metal barrel sat under the drainpipe capturing rain from the roof above the kitchen window. Sadly, too often we'd hear about a young child drowning in one of these barrels when their curiosity got the best of them. Eventually the Council removed all the barrels from the backyards.

Yellow and turquoise budgies flitted about in the aviary the Old Man built across from the chicken hutch. Mother's washing line, attached at one end to a cement post two steps from the back door, stretched almost the length of the middle of the yard. A narrow concrete path protected Mother's slippered feet from the muddy ground when she hung out the washing.

Mother would spend hours washing clothes, bent over the cast iron claw-foot bathtub, with just a rag or two to protect her bony knees from the cold cement floor. Up and down against the ribbed wooden washboard she'd methodically scrub the mountain of soaked laundry. The bar of green laundry soap was so large it would often slip from her grasp, and plop into the tub.

Her hands would turn red from the scalding water she'd poured from the gas heater. They'd turn to blue when she'd rinse the sheets, from five beds, in the frigid water pouring from the single bathtub tap. Her nails were worn down to the skin on the tips of her fingers. Mother would wring as much water out of the washing as she could before lugging an overflowing tin tub into the yard to press the rest of the water out with the hand-turned mangle. I liked helping with the mangle. I'd heave the saturated clothes out of the tub and push them between the two wooden rollers, straining to turn the mangle handle just enough to grip the clothes. With two hands I'd struggle to keep the rollers turning until the pressed washing oozed out on one side as flat as a plank, and water gushed out the other.

Saturday mornings, my sisters Sheila and Doris, and I, took turns at the kitchen sink washing our own underwear, and other personal clothing made from cotton, wool or other natural fibers—synthetics weren't widely available. To whiten our cotton underwear we boiled them in a saucepan on the gas stove. When I reached the age of menstruation, I'd be mortified when I couldn't boil the blood stains out of my knickers. I'd double them over on the washing line and peg them close to the house, out of sight of the neighbors. Our woolen jumpers and cardigans were handled with care—no rubbing, just gentle squeezing. We'd string an old pair of nylons through the arms of the garment to avoid leaving clothes peg marks on the shoulders when we hung them on the line to dry.

Even in mid-summer it wasn't uncommon for the rain to start just as we finished hanging out the clothes, and after one of us struggled to lift a line full of washing with the long wooden prop. If it was a light rain, we'd leave the clothes out, hoping it would blow over. A heavier downpour meant we'd run down the yard pulling the washing off the line as clothes pegs flew in all directions. We'd help Mother hang the dripping articles inside on string lines, which fogged up the windows and turned the kitchen into a smelly, damp steam room.

One dry, breezy day Mother and I stood next to each other on the concrete back door step admiring our billowing line of washing, and scrutinizing those of our neighbors whose wedge-shaped backyards joined ours. Mother's white washing was the whitest. It was a source of great pride to her.

"Look at that," she whispered, tutting as she pointed to a pair of baggy knickers flapping in the wind on a neighbor's line. The once white bloomers were a dingy grey—a cardinal sin in my mother's eyes.

"Fudge"

A soot-stained chimney pot crowned the slate roof of our red brick council house, and all the identical two-story homes in the circle of Mannock and Henshaw Roads. A cement shelf, jutting above the outside of our front door, was just wide enough to protect a visitor from the incessant rain. Every four or five years the Council repainted the exterior wood of the doors, window frames and the front gate, either brown or green. Our house was green—fitting for an Irish family.

Tenants were forbidden by the Council to make changes to the outside of the houses—not that anyone could afford to back then—but they were free to decorate the inside. Mother changed our living room wallpaper so often I'd frequently think I'd wandered into the wrong house.

The interior floor plans were identical. Back doors led into small kitchens. I'd often sit at our kitchen table doing my homework as the grey light filtered through Mother's lace curtains on the sash window. Chipped tea mugs sat upside down on the ribbed, wooden draining board which sloped into a porcelain sink below the window. Above the sink was a single cold-water tap with exposed pipes which stretched to the ceiling, then disappeared into the wall of the bathroom on the opposite wall.

The bathroom was just a room with a bath, no toilet. The bathtub, used for doing the laundry as well as bathing, sat on a cement floor, inches away from the large metal gas water heater known as the copper.

Sunday night was bath night. If you were young enough, you bathed in the metal tub beside the warm coal fire in the living room—otherwise it was the unheated, freezing cold bathroom. To add to the spa-like ambience, for years there was a hole in the bathroom window. A rag had a permanent home there, but it didn't stop the wind whistling through. Nobody languished in the bathtub.

The lavatory—or the lav—as we called it, was attached to the side of the house, but could only be entered through an outside door in the backyard. The small whitewashed room contained a pull-chain flush toilet, and no sink. Washing hands after using the toilet was a routine first introduced by our school teachers. There was no electric light in the lav, which made a trip to the toilet something to be avoided as long as possible when the sun went down.

If anyone had to go during the night they used the chamber pot, known as the "po"—which looked remarkably like a bucket at our house. Stains on the living room ceiling below the bedrooms, were evidence someone hadn't emptied the full bucket when Mother told them. My brothers would get their ears clipped when they waited too long to find the bucket, and were caught peeing out of their upstairs bedroom window. I thought it was preferable to their peeing in the kitchen sink.

The fire in the downstairs living room was the sole source of heat in our two-story house. There was a small fireplace in Mother's bedroom, and one in the corner of the girls' front bedroom, but these were only lit when someone was ill in bed. In those instances, Mother, or the Old Man, would carry shovels full of burning coals up the stairs to start the fire.

A coal man, covered from the top of his cap to his boots in coal dust, would deliver hundred weight sacks of coal to our door. He'd amble to the back of the lorry that had slowly pulled to a stop at the curb, reach over his shoulders and heave the blackened sack full of coal onto his back. A leather flap fixed to the back of his cap stopped the coal dust from going down his neck. Bent almost in half, he'd lug the sack down the front garden path, and around the side of the house, then staggered up the back doorstep into the kitchen. Edging by the kitchen table and chairs, the coalman dumped the contents of the sack with a crash onto the cement floor of the small dark room known as the coal hole, leaving behind a rising cloud of coal dust for us to inhale.

Any kid unlucky enough to be in the living room when the fire died down would be ordered to fetch the coal. I always hoped there would be a pile of small chunks of coal left in the coal hole from the last fire tender. If there were, then I wouldn't need to lift the heavy sledge hammer to smash the huge lumps into sizes I could lift and carry on the shovel to the fireplace.

Across from the coal hole was the kitchen pantry large enough to walk into. No family I knew had a refrigerator. The marble slab bottom shelf stayed cool enough in the mild English summers to keep food from spoiling. There were never any leftovers from our meals, but Mother did save the solidified fat from the weekly roast beef. It was known as "dripping." With a little salt sprinkled on top, bread and dripping made a cheap, savory alternative to bread and butter sprinkled with sugar, which was often all we had for our evening meal.

The top shelf in the pantry, which I could only reach if I stood on the bottom shelf, was where Mother kept important papers and things she wanted to keep secret.

"Go and look on the top shelf," my mother said to me the afternoon of my ninth birthday.

I could see the roller skates before I could reach them. I shrieked with delight. Now I could skate with my friend Diane, who lived across the street. My skates were a little different from her skates. Hers had rubber wheels and shiny brown leather straps. My skates had metal wheels with no straps. Mother cut two pieces of strings to tie the skates to my ankles. As Diane glided noiselessly down Mannock Road, I followed behind, clinging to the wooden garden fence railing with both hands as the metal wheels of my skates scraped against the cement pavement. I don't know if it was the skates, or my lack of balance, but I never learned how to roller skate. If I had learned, I might have been tempted to follow Diane down the middle of the road, and be forced to jump over the horse manure left in the street by the milkman's mare before the avid rose gardeners had time to scoop it up.

Milkmen, in their white jackets, peeked caps, and navy and white striped aprons, delivered milk by horse and cart before most families were awake. Empty bottles, rinsed and left on the front door step, told the milkman how many full bottles to leave. Mother would sit the bottles in a saucepan of cold water on the pantry floor to prevent the milk from spoiling in the summer. Milk wasn't homogenized, so Mother could skim the cream off the top for a special treat over fresh strawberries.

A two-burner gas cooker, with an eye-level grill, used to toast our bread sat on stubby metal legs outside the pantry door. It was years before I found out most people toasted their bread on both sides.

Mother was forever entering the kitchen asking, "Do you smell gas?" which sent everyone in the house sniffing around like bloodhounds.

Gas was used for more than cooking. Mother rushed in the back door one day after gossiping over the hedge with Mrs. Cook. Her face was drawn.

"It's Mrs. Williams," she said. "She put her head in the gas oven. It was that bastard of a husband. He said she was mad and kept putting her in the loony bin. He just wanted her out of the way so he could be with his fancy woman."

Mrs. Williams was a neighbor who'd been released from St. Crispins, a mental asylum, just days before. She talked non-stop and would frequently pop in to gossip with Mother. My sister, Sheila, and I would sit together in the easy chair by the window facing the door between the living room and the kitchen. Mrs. Williams would say, "tadah Bette," to my mother and start to leave, then quickly poke her head back around the living room door and talk some more, then she'd say "tadah Bette" again, leave, and then return. Sheila and I would stifle our laughter as we made a game of counting how many times Mrs. Williams said goodbye, and then returned.

I thought of Mrs. Williams when, years later, after learning about a relative's suicide, I was drawn to a *New York Times Magazine* article by Scott Anderson, entitled, "The Urge to End It All." In the piece he revealed an interesting fact: ". . . one of the most remarkable discoveries about suicide and how to reduce it occurred utterly by chance." Scott was referring to an event known as the, "the British coal-gas story." There was a time when about half the suicides in Britain—2,500 people each year—chose gassing as a method of suicide. As a young child I would often hear, so and so, "put her head in the gas oven." It was almost always a woman. The article explained the gas, back when Mrs. Williams died, was made from coal and highly toxic—it could asphyxiate a person in minutes. A remarkable thing happened when the government switched from coal gas to natural gas—suicides declined dramatically. Unfortunately the change came too late to save Mrs. Williams.

WHAT'S A MULATTO?

From the below-ground flats on a dingy street most people avoided, even in the daytime, would appear men with skin as black as coal—the whites of their eyes splashed with red. They were immigrants from the West Indies, and were among the few non-white faces I ever saw. Some would nod, and give me a knowing smile—recognizing a member of the tribe I suppose.

"Don't look at them," one of my friends would warn, as she grabbed my arm to protect me whenever we passed by them. She needn't have worried, I was already traumatized.

"We'd swap the words 'black man' for the scary bogeyman who was coming to get you," my older sister, Sheila, once told me. "You'd run screaming, and hide under the kitchen table."

I envied my friend Dawn, who was an only child. She and I were the same age, and the same racial mix. Like me, Dawn's father was a long-gone black American soldier. Dawn's mother later married Mr. Baker, an Englishman, who reared Dawn as his own child.

The Bakers lived on Gilletts Road, just up the hill from our house, and across the street from a row of private houses. The group of houses where Dawn lived was called "prefabs"—short for prefabricated metal. These flat-topped bungalows were built by aircraft companies, and some were made from salvaged aircraft and assembled by German POWs. The British wartime Prime Minister, Winston Churchill, promised to build 300,000 of these houses for the returning soldiers. With his usual oratory flair, he pledged, "As much thought will go into the prefabricated housing programme as went to the invasion of Africa." About half as many prefabs were built as were pledged, and they were only supposed to last ten years. They were still occupied four decades after the war, many families refusing to leave them.

The outside of these prefabs looked like tin huts; not nearly as attractive as the brick house we lived in. Inside, they were a lot more modern than our house. They had running hot water, central heating, an indoor bathroom with a toilet, and a kitchen with built-in cupboards. Our house had none of these things.

I flew up the hill to the peace and comfort of Dawn's prefab every chance I could. One day, as we sat on the floor of Dawn's living room, playing with her dollhouse, I heard an unfamiliar sound.

"What's that clicking noise?" I asked.

Dawn stopped playing with her doll and listened. Then she smiled.

"It's just the clock, silly," she said.

We had a clock ticking on the mantelpiece at our house, when it wasn't in the pawn shop—I'd just never heard it above the constant din.

Dawn's parents, Mr. and Mrs. Baker, seemed happy—often joking with each other—something I'd never seen between Mother and the Old Man. I didn't know if Dawn's dad had a speech impediment, but I had trouble understanding a word he said. Mrs. Baker, on the other hand, responded to his mumblings with fits of laughter. Dawn and I would look at each other, amused, and bewildered.

Dawn didn't talk about it, but when she left the confines of her protective home, I'm sure she was subjected to some of the same cruel taunts I suffered. Kids I didn't know would yell out, "Blackie," from across the street. Some would throw stones. I was hurt and confused. When the racial torments became too painful to bear, I'd run home crying and shout at Mother, "I wish I'd never been born." She may have had the same feeling, but she said nothing. I'd see a pained look cross her face once in a while, but there was never a hug, or a sympathetic word.

I'm not sure whether it was Dawn or me who first heard the word "mulatto." We must have been at Dawn's house when we flicked through the pages of a dictionary to see what it meant—there was no such book in our house. In fact there were no books in our house at all. The only reading material were the weekly *Dandy* and *Beano* comics, which we kids wrestled each other for the minute they came through the front door letter box, and the salacious *News of the World*, filled with crime stories and sex scandals earning the newspaper the nicknames of "News of the Screws" and "Screws of the World."

My small finger followed the words in the dictionary and I read out loud, "mulatto—a person who has one black parent and one white parent." Dawn and I looked at each other in the astonished way some kids do. We had a name—a special name. I thought "Mulatto" sounded exotic—certainly better than "Blackie."

Like the rest of the five year olds in the neighborhood, Dawn and I attended Croyland Infant School, a one-story brick building with an iron gated entrance just down the street from my house.

Unlike Dawn, who was well behaved, I spent most of my school days either bent over Headmistress Miss

Swan's knee getting spanked, or facing the wall in the corner of her office. One particular morning, I kicked a teacher in the shins, fled from the school, and ran up Henshaw Road to my house. Mother dragged me back to school and told the teachers to stop picking on me, thereby assuring my bad behavior would continue for several more years. I became notorious. Several school friends told me I was the topic of conversation at their tea tables. "What did Pauline Behan do today?" curious parents would ask.

In addition to the loving parents that properly socialized Dawn, she had a slew of doting aunts. Some were actual relatives—her mother's sisters—and others were her mother's close friends. An endless parade came to visit. There was Auntie France, and Auntie Rose—the relatives—and Auntie May, Auntie Clarice, and Auntie Mary—the friends. These aunts lavished Dawn with affection and gifts. Some of this good stuff sprinkled onto me—a wonderful thing since both affection and presents were in short supply at my house. I was lucky to have a friend like Dawn, and even luckier to find a special aunt of my own.

AUNTIE MARGARET

Each morning, I waited for Auntie Margaret to appear and for our ritual to begin. I was three or four years old and visiting a neighbor by myself. I'd sit on her cold, concrete, front door step, the damp seeping into my thin cotton knickers. I passed the time wiping away the dew collected on the silver foil bottle top of the pint of milk delivered earlier by the milkman.

Sometimes small gangs of scruffy boys in short trousers would shout from across the street, "Oy, Blackie," and follow the greeting with a shower of stones they'd picked up off the road.

The door would open at last, and Auntie Margaret would appear. "Why didn't you knock?" she'd always say in her soft voice as she picked up the milk bottle.

Like a grateful stray cat, I'd jump up and follow her into the warmth and quiet of her home. I'd watch as she put the kettle on. Even now, after so many years, the sound of a whistling kettle reminds me of those cozy mornings making tea, "the proper way,"—as my mother used to say—with loose-leaf Brooke Bond tea. A colorful cloth cozy kept the pot warm while we waited for the tea to brew. Auntie Margaret would reach for the long-handled toasting fork hanging on a hook by the open coal fire, and jab a crumpet onto the prongs.

"Don't hold it too close," she'd caution me. Together

"Fudge"

we'd sit by the fire sipping tea, now cooled with the fresh morning milk, and sweetened with sugar lumps. We devoured the delicious crumpets before the butter we'd spread on them had time to melt.

"Have you ever seen Auntie Margaret's husband?" my mother asked one day. I hadn't. I did hear Auntie tell someone her husband ate eggshells, which I thought was strange. I knew she had a teenage daughter, Shirley, because I'd met her when she visited Auntie Margaret. Auntie and I never talked about why Shirley didn't live with her, or even where Shirley lived. Shirley appeared, and then disappeared. My memory is of a girl with clear, pale skin, big dark eyes, and long, black ringlets touching her shoulders.

Sunday was the day Shirley visited her mother, and I was often invited to join them for tea. Auntie Margaret would open the sideboard in her living room and pull out a spotless, white lace tablecloth and matching serviettes. I'd help her place cups, saucers, and plates on the table, including my own delicate teacup with its matching saucer. Auntie would arrange the small triangle cucumber, and fish paste sandwiches, with the crusts removed, on the tiered glass cake stand. She'd center the stand on the table along with plates filled with an assortment of biscuits and individual cakes.

On one of Shirley's visits, she reached for a small iced cake. Auntie Margaret reminded her they had a visitor and I, as the guest, should go first. This lesson in good manners was new to me. I competed for food with my brothers and sisters, and was not familiar with the practice of taking turns.

There were no matching cups and saucers on the tea table at our house. Mother's tea service was comprised mostly of empty Robinson Jam jars. The bottoms of hot pots left their singed imprints on the oilcloth covering the oblong table in the living room. Small holes with browned edges were evidence of burned out cigarettes left propped on the edge of saucers.

One Sunday tea-time, I made my way around the Old Man's chair as he sat in his usual spot at the head of the table, his back to the kitchen door. I clambered up on the straight-back chair between one of my brothers and the Old Man. Mother hovered between the living room and the kitchen, carrying in slices of white bread she'd sliced and stacked on the breadboard. She returned to the kitchen for the stainless steel teapot, and placed it on the table beside a pint bottle of milk and a bowl full of white sugar. Mismatched plates, some with chipped edges, sat on the table in front of us.

Most tea-times we ate bread and dripping, and once in a while we were treated to jam. This particular Sunday we had jam. I sat in my chair trying to avoid looking at the Robinson's Jam trademark—a black doll known as a golliwog. I knew what would happen each time that jar sat on the table. One of my siblings would point at the golliwog, giggle, then point at me.

I didn't like red jam, so as a special treat for me, my mother would buy lemon curd. I wish this childhood memory stopped there, with the sweet sense of feeling special, but it doesn't. For some inexplicable reason, I insisted on trying to pry open the sealed lemon curd jar lid. I held the glass jar against the edge of the table with one small hand, and used a knife to pry open the metal lid with the other hand. The jam jar slipped from my fingers and crashed to the floor. The Old Man backhanded me across the face, and sent me tumbling to the floor. I wasn't sure which hurt the most—the slap across the chops, or the loss of my favorite jam.

"Fudge"

I may have told Auntie Margaret about these episodes of ridicule and cruelty, which could explain why Shirley was kind to me even though her mother gave me preferential treatment. Shirley never said anything cruel to me when we were alone, and didn't correct me when I called her mother, "Auntie," even though we weren't related. She showed no signs of jealousy when Auntie focused the conversation on me, often asking about my ballroom dancing lessons.

Auntie's sister, Mrs. Ethel Church, taught ballroom dancing lessons to young children at the Bees Wing studio in town. Auntie Margaret had arranged for me to have free lessons. A group of children my age, gathered there once a week to shuffle around the slippery wooden floor, in pairs, to the music from a piano, and Mrs. Church's, "Slow, slow, quick, quick, slow."

I often left Auntie Margaret's house looking a lot more elegant than when I arrived. She had a treadle-operated Singer sewing machine with which she created lovely outfits for me. My favorites were a multi-colored dress with an intricate smocked bodice, a pale green coat, and a matching bowler hat Auntie had purchased. Mother gave me a coat hanger of my own to hang up my coat. The other kids had to hang their coats piled on pegs in the hallway.

To finish off my stylish green ensemble, Auntie slipped a small drawstring leather bag onto my wrist and tucked a perfumed handkerchief inside.

"Ladies always carry a scented handkerchief," she reminded me before we took off for a stroll, hand-in-hand.

"I have to go to the hospital," Auntie Margaret whispered to me one day.

"Can I come?"

"A hospital is no place for little girls," she answered.

Auntie Margaret never came back.

Mother and I went to the funeral service, but I was too young to comprehend the permanence of Auntie Margaret's absence. Each morning I wandered over to her cottage, sat on the cold cement doorstep, waiting for the door to open. Mother would come and take me home.

Years later, a woman who looked like Aunt Margaret—same gentle eyes and soft brown hair—moved into a vacant house nearby. Even though I was old enough by then to have accepted Auntie Margaret's death, I followed this woman down the street to get a better look at her—still hoping.

I've often wondered how different my childhood would've been had Auntie Margaret lived. She treated me as if I were someone special, not just different. Our teatimes together were elegant—linen tablecloths and sparkling china. She swapped my scruffy clothes for the colorful dresses she'd sewn just for me. Our time together was short, but it created an indelible memory which sustained me when I needed a safe place to go.

PRESSS BUTTON "A"

When the snow came, the Old Man would sit rocked back on two legs of an old wooden chair—his long limbs, clad in grimy navy-blue overalls, stretched up on the tall black iron guard encircling the blazing coal fire.

"Pauline," he'd say. "Go up and tell 'em I'm too ill to come to work."

"Go up," meant I was to go up the street, and across the road to the red public telephone box on the corner, and telephone his lie to the British Railway. I couldn't use a neighbor's phone because no family on our street had a telephone in their house. Sometimes I had to queue up outside the public phone box in the freezing cold and wait my turn. I was a kid, so I didn't have the nerve to rap on the telephone box window to remind the caller in front of me to hurry up.

I was proud the Old Man chose me to make such an important phone call, when he had three older kids he could have asked. It wasn't a simple task. At least it wasn't for me. I had to stand on my tiptoes to reach the receiver, and the whole process required a level of coordination which challenged most adults. While I held the large black telephone receiver in one hand, I inserted three large pennies, the size of small pancakes, in the coin slot, and then dialed the phone number. This was the 1950s, and pennies were much larger, and heavier, before the

British Government adopted decimal currency in the 1970s.

When the British Railway person answered, I pushed in a large button, marked with an "A," to connect. Timing was important. I had to wait long enough to make sure it was the British Railway on the other end before I pressed the button. If I pressed too soon, then found out I'd misdialed, I'd lose my money and be afraid to go home. If nobody answered I could press the button marked, "B," and get my money back.

The Old Man called on me to do other important things—like filling out forms for the government.

"Get up here," he'd say motioning to the vacant chair at the living room table where papers were spread out. He'd point to one.

"I want you to read that to me and sign my name at the bottom."

I realize now he may have grown up reading and writing only Irish, and couldn't read or write English.

There were rare intimate moments. The Old Man would take my hand as we strolled to town. He didn't care about much, so I'd imagine the curious looks he got, striding hand-in-hand with a brown-skinned child, didn't concern him at all.

He'd let me crawl up on his lap as he sat in a chair in the living room. I'd comb what little hair he had, and he trusted me to cut the hairs sprouting out of his nostrils and ears.

Mother and the Old Man were heavy smokers who often preferred to smoke rather than eat. There were times we were so broke, there wasn't enough money for even a packet of five cigarettes. At these times, the Old Man would grab a couple of us kids, thrust an empty tobacco tin in our hand, and shove us out the door to look for tippers.

Heads down, we'd go searching the gutters of the neighborhood where smokers tossed the ends of their cigarettes. We were too young to be ashamed and made the tipper hunt a game. We'd compete to see who could collect the most cigarette ends, and compare the sizes.

"Look at this big one," I'd shout, holding it up. We'd wonder who'd tossed such a prize. Tins full, we'd return them to the Old Man. He would slit open the cigarette ends and fill his larger tin full of the loose tobacco.

"Can I roll one?" I'd plead.

He'd nod and I'd climb up on his lap. I'd lay a delicate small paper square between the two black cigarette rollers and sprinkle the loose tobacco along the length of the paper, then squeeze the rollers together, turning the paper around the tobacco. I'd lick the end of the paper on the final turn to seal it. The Old Man would pinch one end of the cigarette to hold in the tobacco, and place it between his lips. He'd take a match from his Swan Vestas matchbox, and strike it on the bottom of his boot. As he lit the cigarette, it flared up at the tip and burned 'til it reached the tobacco. I didn't mind picking up the tippers, and I enjoyed rolling the Old Man's cigarettes, but there was another job I hated.

The gas and electricity to most houses was controlled through coin-operated meters. Each silver shilling piece inserted into the meters allocated a specific amount of the utility. There were times when my brothers, and sisters, and I, would be huddled around the black and white telly watching one of our favorite shows, such as *Filming Africa*. This documentary series, hosted by Armand and Michaela Denis, mesmerized us—the couple lovingly fondled animals that would normally make a person run in the opposite direction. All too often, it would be at a particularly tense moment that the electricity would go off. We'd all groan. Mother would light a match and fumble around trying to find a coin to put in the meter. Most of the time, she didn't have a shilling piece in her purse. If she had enough change she'd hand it to one of us to exchange for a shilling with one of the neighbors. If she had no money, she'd send us to the Shaw's house.

Mrs. Shaw, Marion to mother, was one of the neighbors who often popped into our house to gossip. Marion was a plump woman, who, unlike my mother who dyed her hair black, let her short hair go grey. She didn't wear makeup, and had smooth shiny skin and a cheerful disposition. Harold, her husband, was short, and quiet. His docile nature may have contributed to their happy marriage since Marion liked to talk. The couple had three children—Kathleen, who'd married and moved away, Judith, and son Vincent. Harold's parents lived with them.

I'd never known a grandparent, so I was intrigued by Grandpa Shaw, known with affection by all as "granddad." I never saw granddad dressed in anything more causal than a dark wool suit, white cotton shirt buttoned to the neck, but no tie. The suit had a matching waistcoat from which dangled a gleaming, silver, pocket watch chain.

Mother said granddad had money, and she sometimes gave me a note to give to him. Grandad would read the note, and then hand me extra money along with the shilling for the meter. Grandma Shaw wasn't as visible. Mother told me she was poorly, and when Grandma did answer my knock at their back door, she smelled a little of pee.

Mrs. Shaw was proud of her children and insisted on their being called "by their proper names"—Kathleen not

"Fudge"

Kathy, Judith not Judy, and woe betide those girls at the gate who called out for the good-looking "Vinnie." I was friends with Judith for a short time, and when I was fifteen, we made our first trip to London together.

When we weren't borrowing shillings for the meters, we were making them. Somebody discovered a ha'penny, which was worth one twenty-fourth of a shilling, was slightly larger than a shilling. The Old Man, never one to shy away from something dishonest, would bring out a large metal file and a cup of water, and put one of us to work filing down the copper ha'penny until it was the size of a shilling, and could fit into the electric or gas meter. I detested this job. The copper coin grating on the iron file made my teeth hurt.

I was home one afternoon when the electric man arrived to empty the meter. Mother let him in through the front door. He was dressed in the smart uniform of the Electric Company. The electric meter was in a small cupboard on the wall by the front bay window. The electric man busied himself unlocking the meter and emptying its contents onto the living room table.

Most people looked forward to having their meter emptied. It doubled as a piggy bank. When the meter was full, the shillings added up to more than the electricity purchased, and the customer received a cash rebate.

I'd watch as the electric man separated the shillings from the filed-down ha'pennies, stacking them in neat piles. The few shillings in the meter didn't even come close to paying for the electricity we'd used. Nothing was said. The electric man wrote some numbers on a piece of paper and handed Mother a bill. The same illegal practice was repeated against the gas company. My parents' cavalier attitude toward paying for goods and services extended beyond the utility companies.

The Turnell family owned a grocery shop in Dale Street.

"Here's the list," Mother would say as she thrust the corner of an envelope and a shopping bag at me. "And don't break the eggs," she'd call after me. "And take the bike. It'll be quicker."

We had two bicycles, a boy's bike and a girl's bike. The boy's bike was the Old Man's transportation when he decided to go to work. The girl's bike, shared by eight kids, was black in the places it wasn't rusted, and had no brakes. An advantage to living at the top of Mannock Road was I could hoist myself onto the bike, and gain some momentum before I needed to start peddling. This was an enormous help because the bike was much too big for me. I had to reach up to grasp the handlebars. I was either too little, or too weak, to push the pedals in a full circle, and could only complete half circles. I never knew what clock my mother was watching when she decided my taking the bike made my trip to the shop quicker.

After what seemed like an eternity, I'd arrive at the grocery shop. Mr. Turnell would reach down over the counter to take my shopping bag and the grocery list which Mother had scribbled on an envelope corner. He would fill the bag with staples such as Heinz baked beans, and a packet of Brooke Bond tea. He'd weigh the potatoes and the Brussel sprouts, cut, weigh, and wrap the cheese, and place the six eggs on the very top, along with a packet of five Woodbine cigarettes. My response to Mr. Turnell's outstretched hand was the same: "Mum said she'll pay you next week."

Mr. Turnell would look at me over his glasses. "Your mum already owes me money from last week," he'd say. Then he'd click his tongue and hand me the bag full of groceries. I'd hook the heavy grocery bag on one side of

"Fudge"

the handlebar, and managed to keep the bike upright as I began my journey home. I'd wobble from gusts created by lorries whizzing by me down the busy Croyland Road. I dreaded making the turn from Croyland to Henshaw Road. While doing half turns on the pedals, my left hand on the handlebar, and signaling with my right, my teeth would chatter as I made a frantic right turn across the intersection to the safety of the less-traveled Henshaw Road.

"What kept you?" my mother would ask as I stumbled, weak-kneed, into the house, relieved to have cheated death once more. "What did Mr. Turnell say?" my mother would inquire as she unpacked the grocery bag in the kitchen.

"He said we owed him from last week."

"I'll give him a couple of bob, next week," she'd say matter-of-factly, as she turned toward the gas stove to light up her Woodbine cigarette.

There were times, too, when Mother couldn't afford to have the chimney swept. More than one house went up in smoke from a dirty chimney, so it was left to the Old Man to do the job. I was disappointed when this happened. I looked forward to seeing the chimney sweep. He'd ride up to the house on his bike, loaded down with brushes, rods, a sack for the soot and a shovel to scoop it up. He looked a lot like the coalman, only he was covered from head to toe in soot instead of coal dust.

Mother had cleared a path for him from the front door to the fireplace, and covered the furniture with sheets. I'd watch as the sweep did his job fastening rods to the black-bristled brush and adjusting a cloth over the front of the fireplace to keep as much soot out of the room as possible. The chimney sweep would tell us kids when it was time to go outside. We'd make a mad dash out of the back door, around the side of the house, and into the street where we could get a good view of the roof. We'd let out a collective cheer when the bristles on the long-handled brush burst out of the chimney pot like a stiff black umbrella.

One Sunday evening, while we were taking our baths, Mother opened the tiled door of the small oven next to the fireplace. The oven was no longer used to cook food, and Mother kept our nightclothes, and the girls' liberty bodices—thick cotton vests worn under clothes—inside the oven to keep them warm. Earlier that day the Old Man had swept the chimney. He did such a thorough job removing all the soot and creosote that he caused the oven to become red-hot. When Mother pulled our nightgowns and pajamas out of the oven, we were shocked to see everything scorched.

Mother kept up her fire insurance payments despite being careless about paying her other bills. The insurance company paid her claim with enough money to replace our burnt night clothes. It could've been a coincidence, but after that, each time our nightclothes needed replacing, the Old Man swept the chimney.

Although she had to scrape, beg, and borrow to take care of us, Mother managed to keep her sense of humor. She was amused by the simplest things. The neighbors across the street had two daughters—one slim, and one named Janet who my mother referred to as, "would you look at that." Janet's father was about half the size of his daughter, both in length and breadth. Each week-day morning he'd give Janet's bike a push to get her off to work. He'd grasp what little leather was exposed at the back of the saddle, and make a valiant effort to give his daughter a running start. For some unknown reason, the bicycle faced uphill rather than down. The laws of physics were alive and well, and Janet barely budged.

"Pauline, quick, get over here," my mother would say. She'd be bent over in her favorite spot, peering through the white net curtains in the living room bay window. "Take a look at this," she'd laugh, between the drags on her cigarette. "Can you believe the eejit," she'd sputter, as Janet's father made repeated attempts to launch his daughter. A cigarette, a cup of tea, and live entertainment through the white net curtain—what more could Mother want? Well, for one thing she needed more money, and we kids were expected to pull our weight.

Inside of a British Phone booth
circa 1950

PART TWO

Work, Play, School

SPUD BASHING AND OTHER
MONEY MAKERS

I'm sure there were child labor laws in England in the 1950s, but they must not have applied to farm workers. At eight years old I spent my school summer holidays working in the fields. Armed with a bag lunch of bread with cheese spread, a packet of crisps, a flask of tea, and a bucket, several of my brothers and sisters, and I, would trudge a mile in the early morning cold to an area on the outskirts of town known as Broad Green. We'd hoist ourselves into the bed of the farmer's open lorry, and then, along with an assortment of adults, we'd rumble off over the bumpy roads to the potato fields.

After we arrived at the farm, and half fell out of the back of the lorry, the farmer would size us up and designate a length of a potato row, known as a "stretch," he thought we could handle. The tractor, with a spinner attached, would maneuver down the rows of green leaves and spin the potatoes from under the dirt and lay them on the surface. Each person, with back bent, would walk the length of the stretch, dragging a bucket to scoop up the potatoes. The filled buckets would be emptied into a burlap sack until it was full.

I felt a sense of pride after I filled a sack. Pride would turn to panic, though, if I saw the spinner coming down my row before I had picked up the previous load of potatoes. I was also afraid of the adults who would stand at the top of the field with their hands on their hips, glaring at me, and any other kid, who held up the spinner. Working in the fields was their livelihood, and they were already ticked off at having us kids in the field taking money away from them. I also knew, from past experience, that if I couldn't handle my stretch the farmer would shorten it up. I often had trouble keeping up with the spinner. My twelve-year-old sister, Sheila, who only had one arm, but who'd managed to pick up all her spuds, would come to my rescue. We'd both scramble like mad, picking up the potatoes as fast as we could to get out of the path of the oncoming tractor.

After a rain storm, my task became even more challenging. I could barely lift my legs as I trudged down the stretch dragging my bucket, the field mud caked to the bottom of my welligogs. At the end of the day, the wet dirt turned out to be a blessing. The mud that stuck to my boots and bucket, also stuck to the potatoes, and helped tilt the scales in the right direction when the sacks were weighed. The farmer paid us one token for each sack of potatoes. We'd have to wait until the end of the week to exchange these for cash—the farmer's way, I suppose, of making sure he had a work crew for at least a week.

At lunchtimes the field would grow quiet. The air filled with the fragrance of the dark tilled soil. I'd sit on my upturned bucket, and on dry days, get to feel the warmth of the sun on my face as I ate my cheese spread sandwich, which somehow tasted better than it did at the kitchen table.

At the end of the work week, I stood in line waiting for the farmer to count real money into my outstretched hand. We knew Mother's hand would also be open when we kids jostled our way through the back door. Knowing this, once we scrambled off the lorry in Broad Green, my siblings and I would make a mad dash for Percy Brown's shop, and fill up with sweets before heading home.

Most evenings we'd keep Mother supplied with potatoes we'd hidden in our buckets. She'd reward us with plates of golden-brown chips that we'd smother in salt and vinegar.

When potato-picking season was over there were peas to pick—or the pea-picking could have come first. Either way, I became the laughing stock of the pea-picking field my first year. "I'm never going to fill a sack at this rate," I moaned to one of my brothers. His sack was half full and mine looked empty. He peered into my sack and doubled over with laughter. Instead of tossing in the whole pod I'd spent the morning shelling the peas into the sack.

Summer holidays, if you could call them "holidays," flew by.

"I'll be shut of ye soon, thank Christ," said Mother, as she tried to quiet the living room full of fighting kids. By early September we were all back in school and two months later the whole neighborhood began preparing for Guy Fawkes Night, a celebration of sorts, held on November the fifth each year. A week before the fifth, I'd help my siblings stuff crumpled-up newspapers into a frayed shirt, and a worn pair of trousers, fashioned a head from a burlap sack and slapped on a hat. We'd stick this scarecrow-looking thing in a pushchair, hang a sign around its neck with the words: "Please spare a penny for the guy," and push it around the neighborhood rattling a tin can. The pennies we'd collect were used to buy fireworks.

The Old Man stacked anything burnable onto a huge bonfire in the back garden, just like all the other dads. We'd toss potatoes in their jackets into the fire to cook, and run around the yard twirling sparklers. My favorite firework was the spinning Catherine wheel—a pinwheel named after St. Catherine of Alexandria. Every year the Old Man nailed one to the outside of the backyard toilet door leaving an indelible scorched imprint.

The finale of the evening included burning the "Guy" on the top of the bonfire while we all sang:

*"Please to remember
the fifth of November
Gunpowder, treason, and plot,
We see no reason why gunpowder season
should ever be forgot"*

Only after taking history in school did I learn our fundraising guy was an English Catholic nobleman who, on November 5, 1605, plotted to blow up the Houses of Parliament during the State Opening. The plan was to kill King James I, with the goal of restoring a Catholic monarchy. An anonymous tip to a Catholic Lord, warning him not to attend the opening, cast suspicion.

The search was on, and Mr. Guy Fawkes was discovered lurking beneath the House of Lords with a suspicious cache of gunpowder. He was arrested and later hanged. Guy's thwarted plot has been memorialized in England for over 400 years by burning Guy in effigy, accompanied by exploding gunpowder, known as fireworks. Once I understood what Guy Fawkes Night was all about, it seemed macabre, to say the least, but it didn't lessen my enjoyment.

November gave way to December with snowmen on each corner, snowball fights, icy pavement slides, and Christmas caroling—one of our top money-makers. My sister, Doris, and I coaxed our younger brother, Kevan, to

"Fudge"

accompany us. His blonde curls and blue eyes made him the perfect singing angel. The three of us chased each other up Gilletts Road passed my friend Dawn's house, to Northampton Road where the rich people lived. I now know these people were barely middleclass, but they were rich compared to us. Both sides of Northampton Road were filled with private homes. When the occupants opened the door, a nosy child could see warm lights, thick carpets, and polished tabletops.

Our carol singing trio was determined to make as much money as possible. As soon as we reached a front door, one of us would ring the doorbell, and we'd begin singing. Sometimes a well-lit house would go dark after we rang the bell. The hint was taken and off we'd scamper to the next house. Everyone who opened the door gave us some money, and some added an extra coin when they spotted Kevan. The generous families were paid return visits each year.

At the end of the evening we'd pull off the socks we'd worn for gloves, sit on the cold cement curb under the faint glow of the gas streetlight, and count our money. It was a good night when bronze threepenny bits and silver sixpences outnumbered the copper pennies. Mother allowed us to keep our carol singing money so we could buy Christmas presents.

Each year, my Christmas gift to Mother was either a manicure set, or a bottle of perfume. I'd purchase both items at the sprawling Woolworth's shop on Market Street, a place I'd wander around for hours. The manicure set consisted of a plastic, black and gold pouch filled with a metal nail file, an emery board, and a pair of small scissors. When Mother unwrapped the gift she'd smile, and look at each of the manicure items as if she'd never seen them before.

One of the last things my mother needed, though, was a manicure set. Most of her finger nails were worn down from the scrubbing board she used to do the weekly wash, bent over the bathtub.

The "Evening in Paris" perfume came in a small purple bottle. Mother would dab a drop on each wrist and behind her ears. I could have imagined this, but when the strong scent hit the air, it wouldn't have been unlike my brothers to shout out, "Poo," and head for the door.

When we weren't outside the house making money, we were inside making it. Thurgar Bolle manufactured hair slides—small clasps girls used to pin back their hair. Boxes of slide parts were delivered to the house and Mother would assign each of us kids a share of the work. We had to complete our quota before we were allowed to go out and play. The task was the kind of detailed, monotonous work which I hated. Piles of decorative pink plastic bunnies were heaped on the living room table. I'd scrape off any excess plastic before assembling the slide. By the time my quota was complete, the tips of my fingers bore an indentation from the pressure it took to attach and secure the pronged metal clip to the pink bunny. The final step was to clip the assembled slide to a card and place it in my assigned box. If it wasn't for my friend, Joy, who pitched in to help me, I might never have left the house any evening.

A trip to Bob Abrams pawn shop, downtown on Pebble Lane, was a sign we were even more desperate for money than usual. My sister Sheila and I would trundle off to town carrying one of two items—either Mother's wide gold wedding band, or the mantelpiece clock. I doubt we got more than a couple of shillings for either item, more perhaps for the ring, but it was enough to put bread and butter on the table until we could cash in the weekly family allowance coupon.

Tea was the one thing that was never in short supply. "Polly put the kettle on," Mother would often call out to me when I ventured into the kitchen. Tea was served from first thing in the morning until last thing at night. With the constant supply of caffeine, I'm surprised anyone managed to get to sleep. "Would you like a cup of tea, love," was the first thing offered to any visitor. "That was a nice cup of tea," was praise indeed from Mother. She was equally quick to tell you, "It tastes like piss," if you poured a cup before it had time to brew.

Brooke Bond Dividend Tea was our favorite brand of loose leaf tea, and it came with a perforated stamp affixed to the outside of the packet for easy removal. If you saved enough stamps to fill a card, about sixty, you could trade it in at a grocery shop for a few shillings.

Early one evening the Old Man gave me a filled stamp card and sent me to Turnell's shop to exchange it for money to buy ten Woodbine cigarettes, and a loaf of bread. I ran all the way to Turnell's, hoping to get back home before dark. I stood on my tiptoes and handed the card over the counter to Mr. Turnell. He opened the card.

"You're missing a stamp," he said.

I must not have heard him because he repeated himself as he returned the card to me. I opened the card and looked in disbelief at the empty square. I knew from past experience if you licked the stamp too much it wouldn't stick to the card.

Is that what happened? Did it fall off?

I left the shop and retraced my steps with my head down, searching for the stamp under the flickering street gaslights, tears blinding my eyes.

I walked all the way back to my house but was afraid to go in. The Old Man would be waiting for his packet of fags and I didn't have them. I sat on the cement curb outside our house crying. I finally got so cold I had to go in. My punishment was either too severe to remember, or mild enough to forget.

Woolworth's Market Street, Wellingborough
Circa 1977

CONKERS ANYONE?

Before I and the other kids in our neighborhood became mesmerized by the flickering images on a television screen, we'd spend every minute we weren't in school outside playing in the street. Girls played hopscotch in the chalked squares outside front gates, and jumped rope in the middle of the road—a road less travelled in those days, since only one family in the neighborhood owned a car.

All you had to do to find a playmate was bang on the door of just about any house in our neighborhood. One afternoon I hopped and skipped down the garden path of my friend who lived next door to the Thompson's. I tapped on the back door—strangers went to the front doors. My friend's dad answered my knock. As he walked back into the house to get his daughter, I heard him call out, "Darkelene is here for you."

At least his name for me rhymed with mine.

On the days when nobody could come out, I played two-ball against the outside wall of our house. When I began learning the game I held one rubber ball in each hand. I'd throw the ball in my right, underhanded against the wall, and at the same time move the second ball in my left hand to my right, and catch the ball which bounced off the wall, with my left. I did this slowly at first. The more I practiced the quicker I became. Instead of having my two hands separated, I could cup them, one above the other, and bounce and catch the balls in one continuous motion. I'd play for hours or until Mother, tired of the noise ricocheting into the kitchen, would yell out the back door, "Pack it in unless you want a clout."

Whether I was skipping, or playing ball, there was always a rhyme to go with any game. My favorite two-ball rhyme was:

> *"Gypsy, gypsy, lived in a tent,*
> *she couldn't afford to pay the rent,*
> *the rent man came*
> *she ran away,*
> *over (a signal to throw one of the balls overhand)*
> *the hills, and far away."*

Actual gypsies would appear in our street from time-to-time. I had no idea the term "gypsy" was a disparaging word, and a more respectful address would have been Romani.

The women wore their long brown hair in plaits, pinned on top of their heads. They carried baskets filled with clothes pegs, ribbons, and other odds and ends. The men walked alongside a horse and cart and shouted out for donations of scrap metal. I believed the tales told about gypsies—they were all thieves, and when they weren't stealing your stuff, they would steal your children. I honestly don't think Mother, or the Old Man, would've cared if a couple of their kids had gone missing.

While I was playing two-ball against the wall, my brothers and their friends might be in the park across the street. During the months of September and October, horse chestnut trees dropped their round prickly green pods. When they hit the ground they'd crack open and

"Fudge"

reveal the hard brown seeds inside, known as conkers. The boys would gather up these conkers, and prepare them for battle. The seeds came in different shapes, and the coveted ones were symmetrical and hard. There wasn't anything the boys could do about the shape, but they could make the conkers harder.

Some days I would come into the kitchen from outside and be overcome by the smell of vinegar. My brothers were soaking their conkers, ready to bake them in the oven. This practice was called cheating by some, but most boys did it.

Before they hardened the conkers, my brothers scrambled to find a nail and a stone to carefully bang a hole in the center without cracking the conker. Sometimes my brother, Billy, would swipe one of Mother's kitchen forks and bend a tine and use it to make the hole. He'd get a clip around the ear for his trouble.

A knotted shoe lace, or in the case of my brothers, a piece of string from one shoe, would be threaded through the hole. I stood in the backyard one afternoon and watched as my brother, Kevan, faced his opponent. It may have been Billy Cripps from across the street, or Dave Sanders who lived in the cul-de-sac, or one of the Hadley twins. There were usually a couple of boys watching. Despite their uniform of knee socks and short pants—they weren't old enough to wear long trousers—they were ready to do battle. Kevan dangled his conker at arm's length. His opponent wound the string on his conker around his hand leaving enough to flick his conker at Kevan's.

I've long forgotten all the rules of the game. But if you cracked your opponent's conker for the first time, your conker was known as a "oner." If you cracked two conkers it was known as a "twoer"—and so on. If you managed to crack a conker with previous wins, then you took on its winning numbers.

I thought playing conkers was a thing of the past until I found out, decades after watching those backyard games, that a conker competition is held in England, in October of each year. It began in 1965 and has grown to become an international event, raising loads of money for charity. Coincidentally, the competition is held in Oundle, a town only 20 miles northeast of Wellingborough.

In the winter, groups of the neighborhood boys would wander the streets swinging flaming tins in circles. Empty Heinz baked beans tins were punched with holes, and tied with string. The insides were filled with soft bark from trees, and then lit. Swirls of light surrounded these roving bands of boys. I never quite understood the attraction.

The kids I grew up with who lived on Mannock and Henshaw Roads were never unkind to me, never called me names. I'm sure they were curious about my appearance, and I would've loved to have heard how their parents explained this difference.

When the autumn and winter days passed and blustery spring days arrived, my brothers and their friends would clutter our kitchen table with old newspapers, string, and tree twigs as they busied themselves with kite making. I'd follow them into the park across the street and watch as one boy would hold the kite, while the other held the ball of string and ran backwards as the kite was let go. Lift off was a challenge. The frame was often too heavy, or the wind wasn't strong enough. Failure didn't seem to deter the boys, and they'd keep trying until cheers rang out celebrating a takeoff.

When they weren't whacking conkers, swinging flaming tins, or flying kites, the boys would turn their attention to tormenting girls. They'd careen down pathways on their trolleys made from baby pram wheels and orange boxes, and with no brakes other than the soles of their shoes. They'd drive us girls screaming from our placid game of hopscotch.

Cherry Knocking was a game boys and girls played together. Someone would be brave enough to knock on a neighbor's front door, then run like a hare and join the rest of the gang behind a hedge some distance away. When the occupant opened the front door and found nobody there, we'd clap our hands over our mouths to smother the laughter. The second time we'd bang on the door, the home-owner would catch on to what was happening and shout out a variety of threats, which only served to send us into louder hysterics.

When it was too wet to play outside I'd content myself with listening to the wireless. To hear above the constant squabbling of my siblings, I'd get as close as possible to the wireless, which sat on the shelf of a low cupboard by the bay window where the pay-as-you-go electric coin meter was housed. I'd stand on the cushion of Mother's easy chair and lean forward, my head resting on my folded arms on the back of the chair. My favorite program was "Meet the Huggets," with actor Jack Warner playing Joe, and Kathleen Harrison playing Ethel. The cockney voices of both actors were comforting to me for some reason.

I imagined Jack Warner to be handsome, and I wasn't disappointed when a few years later, he appeared on the telly as a London Bobby in the serial, "Dixon of Dock Green." He had even features—his nose wasn't too large, and his ears didn't stick out. His hair was neatly trimmed and plastered down with Brylcreem. His mouth lifted on one side in a slight smile.

Our first television arrived in the back of a Manning's van. We had to rent it because we couldn't afford to buy, although renting didn't come cheap. In addition to the weekly payment, Mother had to purchase a television license to pay for commercial-free BBC—the only channel available in the 1950s. All programs were in black and white, and televised for a limited number of hours. On weekdays, the Postmaster General, who was in charge of such things, allowed broadcasting for a couple of hours in the morning. There was no television between six and seven at night so parents could trick their kids into thinking TV had ended for the evening, and they could get them to go to bed without an argument. It was called "toddlers' truce." All programming stopped at 11 pm. On weekends the rules were relaxed a little.

More than once, the Old Man came home from the pub in a foul mood and decided he didn't like seeing us kids sitting on the floor in the living room enjoying a television program.

"Take it back," he'd order my brothers, Terry and Kevan.

Terry was around ten years old, and Kevan three years younger, and the two had to lift the telly into the empty baby pram and haul it back to Mannings' shop—mostly uphill from our house. Kevan told me the shopkeeper would put the television in the corner, and let Kevan know it would be there when he and Terry came to pick it up the next week—the usual pattern.

Somehow Mother managed to scrounge together enough money to send us to the pictures on Saturday mornings. Along with a group of neighborhood kids, I'd pile onto the green double decker bus parked at the bus stop on the corner of Henshaw Road. "Upstairs!" we shouted to each other as we clambered up the steps to the seats reserved for smokers. "Fares please," the conductor called out, and we'd hand over our pennies for a bus ticket. The conductor placed the fare in his leather pouch, turned the crank of the ticket machine, which spat out the ticket.

In addition to the conductor, whose job it was to collect fares and ring the bell for stops and starts, there was the bus driver, and the dreaded Inspector. The Inspector's job was to jump on any bus without warning, usually while it was moving, which I thought was very daring. He'd ask to see our tickets to make sure we'd paid—and to ensure the bus conductor wasn't pocketing the money. I never witnessed anyone being apprehended for crimes against the United Counties Omnibus Company. The constant fear of an unexpected visit by an Inspector kept us all honest.

Mother would give us enough money to get into the pictures, to buy some sweets, and for bus fare back home. If we were lucky we'd get extra money for fish and chips. At times I'd spend my return fare on more sweets, and then have to walk home.

Going to the pictures on Saturday mornings was the highlight of my week. The bus would drop me, and half the kids in the neighborhood, off on Market Street in the center of town, and we'd run down Midland Road to The Lyric Cinema—a fixture since 1936. There were three other cinemas in town: The Palace, The Silver, and The Regal—but the Lyric was the largest, and most attractive of them all. A description on the website "Cinematreasures," reminded me just how grand it was:

"The Lyric Cinema was equipped with a Compton 2Manual/5Ranks organ, which had an illuminated console on a lift, and was opened by organist Neville Turner. Seating was provided in stalls and circle levels. The proscenium was 40 feet wide, the fully equipped stage was 20 feet deep and there were fifteen dressing rooms. The cinema also had a cafe for the convenience of its patrons."

I was enthralled by the films, and enthusiastically joined in the sing-alongs. I may have been a member of the Saturday club for children known as "The ABC Minors"—something the Association of British Cinemas chain (ABC), created. Before the cartoons and films were shown, the words of the "ABC Minors Song" would appear on the screen, and a packed house of kids would sing the ABC song to the tune of "Blaze Away,"—a rousing march:

> "We are the boys and girls well known as
> the Minors of the ABC
> And every Saturday we line up
> to see the films we like and
> shout aloud with glee
> We love to laugh and have a sing-song
> just a happy crowd are we
> We're all pals together
> we're minors of the ABC"

It was a wonderful mad house.

One of my favorite films was the thrilling adventures of *Flash Gordon and the Clay People*. Who'd have guessed space travel, and those doors which magically opened by themselves, would become a reality in our lifetime. Ear-splitting cheers and boos would fill the Lyric, depending on who came on the screen. Cowboys with white hats elicited the cheers, and those with black hats, and the Indians, got the boos. As the excitement built, "Episode 2 next week" would flash across the screen which drew loud groans, followed by deafening boos. After the show ended, we'd dash across the street to the fish and chip shop. A piece of cod, coated in thick batter and deep fried to a golden brown, was topped with a scoop of chips, and cradled in several layers of newspaper. I'd apply copious amounts of salt and vinegar onto the steaming fish and chips. Unable to wait for the food to cool, I'd use my tongue to sling a chip from one side of my mouth to the other, as I made my way up Midland Road to the bus stop on Market Street. I was in heaven.

Decades later I was saddened to learn The Lyric closed to become a bingo hall in 1969, and then was pulled down to make way for a shopping mall in 1975.

Wellingborough currently has no cinemas.

The Lyric Cinema Wellingborough

HE FORGOT TO PAINT THEM

Sunday mornings, Mother rounded up a couple of my siblings, and me, and packed us off to Our Lady's Catholic Church. Our attendance at church had less to do with instilling religious faith, and more to do with Mother's desperate bid for a few hours of peace and quiet. At least she'd be "shut," of a couple of kids for a while.

How righteous I'd feel, standing on my tiptoes as I dipped my finger into the holy water from a stone pedestal basin inside the church door, and made the sign of the cross on my forehead. The church was cold, grey, and quiet. I was captivated by the marble statues of Mary and Jesus, and mesmerized by the images etched in the stained glass windows. I never understood a word of the Latin Mass, but along with my brothers and sisters I'd memorized when to kneel, and when to rise, and would sneak a sideways peek at those in the pew across the aisle to make sure I was in sync.

Sometimes Mother would hand me a note as I was leaving for the long walk to the church.

"Give this to the Father," she'd tell me.

After Mass, I handed over the note to Father Payne. He'd read it, reach inside his robe, and then press a one pound note into my hand. To my knowledge, neither Mother nor the Old Man ever set foot in the church. Mother's half-brother, Jim O'Toole, was a different story.

"Fudge"

Uncle Jim had emigrated from his and Mother's hometown of Castlebar, to work for the Ford Motor Company in Dagenham, Essex, a suburb of East London. It was common for men to leave their families in Ireland to find work in England, and elsewhere—although I never heard Uncle Jim mention a wife or children. Mother reluctantly answered my question about the difference in her maiden name of Halligan, and Uncle Jim's last name of O'Toole.

"We have the same mother," she said. "Jim's father, John O'Toole, died, and his mother married my father, and they had me and your Uncle Tom." Other than finding out my grandmother was a midwife, this was the most information about her parents I'd been able to pry out of my mother. Now I knew why Uncle Jim, who was short, stout, with thinning brown hair, looked nothing like my mother, who was slender, with thick coal-black hair.

Uncle Jim would take the hour-long train ride from London to visit us most weekends.

"Where's Uncle Jim?" I'd ask when I couldn't find him before breakfast on a Sunday morning.

"He took off early. Jim never misses first Mass," my mother would always reply.

I wondered aloud why he'd take the time to walk all the way to Our Lady's Catholic Church when he was just visiting for two days.

"Jim is devout," Mother explained.

I didn't know what, "devout" meant, but it sounded strict.

Each time Uncle Jim visited, he carried a worn, brown leather suitcase tied with string. The suitcase was stuffed with clothes for Mother to wash. When the laundered white shirts had dried, he'd ask me to iron them. I was eight-years-old and proud to be asked to perform such an important task.

The iron was made of heavy metal, and had to be heated on the gas stove in the kitchen. A wad of cloth was bound around the handle to prevent third degree burns. To test the heat of the iron, I'd remove it from the burner, turn it upside down, and spit on the bottom—just like Mother did. I wasn't skilled enough to judge the correct temperature, and I'd scorch the collars of Uncle Jim's shirts. Horrified, I'd try in vain to wipe away the brown streaks, but the rubbing made them worse. Uncle Jim never complained, and continued to ask me to iron his shirts. He'd secretly press a half-a-crown in my hand as he passed me in the kitchen when he left to return home.

During one of Uncle Jim's visits I overhead Mother talking to him in the living room—her voice cracking with emotion. The Old Man came into the room from outside and hung his cap on the nail on the wall. Uncle Jim stood up and faced him.

"You're lower than a snake's belly," he spat at him. The Old Man turned and strode out of the house. It was the only time I ever saw him leave the house without his cap.

My mother's brother, Tom, visited once. He looked just like Mother—slightly built with black hair and very pale skin. Decades later I'd learn Uncle Tom immigrated to America, so he may have come to say goodbye to my mother.

Visits by relatives of the Old Man were rarer still. Only one came to the house—his brother, Bill. Uncle Bill, his wife, Peg, and their three daughters, Joan, Maisie, and Rita, lived in Harrow-on-the Hill in Middlesex, on the outskirts of London. My two older sisters and I paired off with our respective cousins. Joan was my sister Sheila's age, Maisie was my sister Doris' age, and Rita was my age.

"Fudge"

I was fascinated by the cockney accents of our cousins—they sounded like the cheerful, loud-mouthed young men who sold goods in our Wellingborough town market on Saturday mornings. I looked up to my cousins. They lived in London, the capital city, with its palaces, museums, and West End theatres. Our town was small in comparison, and dominated by boot and shoe factories. Our three cousins didn't hesitate to remind my sisters, and me, we were "country." Despite their teasing I looked forward to their visits.

As the six of us sat in a line outside on the street curb one dry afternoon, one cousin asked if we'd like to learn a rhyme. I loved to sing and was probably the first to shout out, "yes." The rhyme went like this:

"God made the little niggers,
He made them in the night,
He made them in a hurry
and forgot to paint them white."

My three cousins and two sisters laughed. I'm sure I cried.

Uncle Bill didn't look, or behave, anything like the Old Man. He was a foot shorter, and good-humored. He didn't talk about his Irish relatives, either, at least not in front of us kids. I never learned anything about his parents, or knew if he and the Old Man had other siblings.

Auntie Peg brought her accordion with her when she visited, and I'd sit cross-legged on the floor next to the fire, fascinated as she moved her chubby fingers up and down the keys, and squeezed the bellows at the same time.

Josephine, whose relationship with Mother and the

Old Man was never disclosed, visited from Ireland. She looked younger than my mother, and was small, slim, with bright red fingernails. Her jet black hair was curly, and long enough to reach below her shoulders. Josephine wore flared, colorful cotton dresses, and makeup. Her fragrant perfume lingered whenever she left a room. Her tiny, backless, high-heeled shoes clicked when she walked on the linoleum floor. I thought she looked like a film star.

One morning Mother called to me from the kitchen. She wore one of her faded wrap-around pinafores, her hair hidden inside a turban, and her usual bedroom slippers with holes cut to provide an exit for each of the swollen corns on her little toes.

"Take a cup of tea up to Josephine," she told me.

Bringing a visitor a cup of tea in bed was a treat reserved for someone special. I managed to get to the top of the stairs without spilling tea into the saucer.

Josephine had spent the night in the large front bedroom where all the girls slept. I steadied the cup and saucer with one hand and pushed open the bedroom door with the other. I was startled to see the Old Man leaning over Josephine, who was lying in bed with her head turned away from him.

"Give us a kiss," I heard the Old Man say.

TOP OF THE MORNIN'

Our house, with two small downstairs rooms, one toilet, and three bedrooms, wasn't large enough for a family of ten, yet somehow we found room for lodgers. Many nights when I'd lay half asleep in bed; the sound of unfamiliar Irish voices would drift upstairs, signaling someone new was in the house. The next morning I'd kick away the rubber hot water bottle, now cold, and push off the pile of coats Mother had spread on the bed to keep my sisters and me warm. Frosty streaks had caked the inside of the sash bedroom windows. I'd shiver my way downstairs hoping the coal fire had been started. What face, I wondered, would appear from under the rumpled covers on the living room couch.

"Top of the mornin' "—would be the usual greeting from another grateful young Irishman whom the Old Man had brought home from the pub the night before.

Although I was just eight or nine years old, I felt the change in our house when we had visitors. It wasn't only the extra money from the lodgers—which may have paid for our Saturday morning pictures—it was that Mother and the Old Man put their quarrels, and their stony silences, on hold. At times we'd have as many as three lodgers living with us, which brought the total occupants of our small house to 13—all sharing one bath, and one outside toilet—an inconvenience I credit with expanding the size of my bladder.

One Friday evening, after a hard week's work digging ditches, Gus, one of the Irish lodgers, was taking a bath. Mother let out a shout when she noticed water seeping under the bathroom door into the kitchen where she was standing. I watched as the Old Man tried to push open the bathroom door, but it wouldn't budge. With two strides, he was outside the back door, and called to Mother to get him a rag. The Old Man wrapped the cloth around his fist. He smashed a hole in the small bathroom window, reached inside the broken glass, unlocked the latch, lifted the sash window, and climbed in. The crowd of on-lookers and I were pushed out of the kitchen into the living room, and the door was closed. Mother told us the rest of the story the next day.

"When the Old Man climbed in the window he found Gus lying on the floor. He'd climbed out of the bath, slipped, and fell on the wet cement floor, and knocked himself out. When he fell, his foot hit the tap on the copper, and the boiling water gushed out. You should see the size of the blisters on his legs."

Mother, who always seemed to know what to do, had cleaned and bandaged the huge bubbles on Gus' feet and legs, saving him from developing a serious infection. The hole in the broken bathroom window was plugged with a rag and remained that way for years.

Two of my favorite lodgers were the brothers, Tom and Jerry. They weren't quite as entertaining as the cat and mouse cartoon duo, but they were a lively pair. Our dilapidated piano had more dead keys than live ones, but Tom managed to bang out a tune, while Jerry accompanied him on the penny whistle. After a night at the pub with the Old Man, the three of them would gather around the piano in the living room and sing their mournful Irish

"Fudge"

songs.

"If you ever go across the sea to Ireland," began one of their favorites. I sang along with them—silently.

One Saturday morning, before a group of us kids left to ride the bus downtown to watch our weekly pictures at the Lyric Cinema, Mother told us both lodgers would be leaving before we got back. I felt sad when the two cartoon characters appeared on the film screen, reminding me I would never again see Tom and Jerry, the lodgers.

Augustus Arthur was another memorable lodger. He was handsome in a traditional Irish way with his dark curls and mischievous light eyes. But he didn't stay long. I overheard Mother talking to our neighbor, Mrs. Cook, over the privet hedge one morning as I sat shivering in the outside lavatory.

"He was arrested by the coppers for carrying an iron pipe," I heard Mother say. I was hoping she wouldn't speak any lower or I wouldn't be able to hear who "he" was. "When he went in front of the magistrate, he was asked why he was carrying an iron bar. 'Your Honor,' " my mother reported, imitating an even thicker Irish accent, " 'there are some violent people on the streets, and you need to protect yourself.' " The judge agreed, and sent Augustus packing.

Mother and Mrs. Cook burst out laughing. Augustus Arthur was on his way back across the sea to Ireland.

YOU SHOW ME YOURS

A blanket of green, flecked with tiny white daisies and yellow buttercups, is my summer memory of Croyland Park. What a gift it was to have such a place to play, just across the street from where I lived.

My friend Dawn and I, two eight-year-olds, would sit cross-legged on the warm grass—our knees almost touching.

"If you see a golden reflection, it means you like butter."

Dawn was repeating the words I'd said to her. We giggled as we held a buttercup under each other's chin. The yellow glow was difficult to see on our caramel-colored skin. Tossing aside the buttercups, we busied ourselves making daisy chains from the wildflowers heaped in the laps of our cotton frocks.

"Oh no," I cried when the tiny slit I'd made in the stalk opened to the end, and I couldn't thread through the next daisy.

"Do it like this," said Dawn as she used her fingernail to make a tiny slit further up the stalk.

"See. Now you can poke in the next daisy."

Our daisy chains completed, we joined the ends to make a circle. Leaning toward each other we placed a crown of white daisies on the top of each other's springy black curls.

Holding onto our daisy crowns with one hand, and carrying our empty jam jars and fishing nets in the other, Dawn and I ran down the hill to the shallow brook which ran the length of the park and beyond. Squatting as close to the edge of the water as I dared, I scooped my net into the muddy water and tipped the wiggling tadpoles into my jar, half-filled with brook water. The jar would eventually join all the others, lined up in our backyard waiting to be kicked over by the dog.

Joy, another childhood friend, lived on my same street, and she and I would sprint to the park to go brook jumping. Joy, with her long legs would always win the race. The same long limbs would vault her across the park brook, as she'd easily sail from one slippery bank to the other. After a running jump, I'd hurl myself across the stream, barely land on the opposite bank, and then slowly slide back into the muddy water. Landing in the brook was a recurring problem for me.

The smelly brook mud would cake to the bottoms, sides, and tops of my white canvas plimsolls, and seep up into my white socks. I'd soak my shoes and socks in the brook and do my best to wash out the mud. The dirty water only made them look worse. I'd wring out as much water as possible, and then bang the plimsolls and socks on the grass to dry them out. The end result would be brown shoes and socks with green grass stains.

I'd tug the soggy shoes and socks back on my cold, wet feet, and pat the stretched tops of the socks against my ankles. For some reason I thought my mother wouldn't notice the stained shoes and socks, or hear the squishing as I crept in the back door. Of course she saw, and she heard, and I got a clip around the ears.

There were other times when Joy and I would brook-jump our way to the far end of the park, known as the "top field." A large black sewer pipe was visible as it crossed the brook, stretching from one side of the bank to the other. The pipe was always wet—even in summer. Joy, of course, traversed the pipe like an expert tightrope walker. I'd wobble my way across, almost make it, and then fall in.

Sometimes I'd go to the park with my first boyfriend, Barry Hicks, who lived just up the street from me near the red phone box. We'd walk hand-in-hand to the top field, but some distance from the brook. Unlike the lower field near the park entrance, the top field wasn't mowed by the local Council and tall grasses turned golden and dry in the summer. Barry and I built a thatched cottage in the field which, to the unimaginative, looked like a clearing in the hedge with dry grass on top. We'd crawl into our cottage and kiss with our mouths closed and our eyes open.

One day Barry invited me to go camping. He'd erected a tent in his backyard. As I rounded the corner of his house, I stopped in my tracks. There, hanging on his mum's washing line was something I'd longed for. A small, white lacy bra was swaying in the breeze. The bra belonged to Barry's sister, Margaret. She and I were close in age and both beginning to develop breasts. My sister, Sheila, had urged my mother to get me a bra.

"Come up," said my mother one day and beckoned me to follow her upstairs. She reached into the top drawer of her bedroom dresser and pulled out one of her plain white cotton bras. Mother had little or no bust but it was still more than I had.

"Put a stitch or two in the cup, and you'll be fine," she instructed.

I did my best to alter the bra so it would fit, but sewing wasn't my strong suit, and the seam could be seen under my clothes. What I wanted was what Barry's sister had—a pretty bra which fitted.

My daydream was interrupted by Barry's voice calling my name. I crawled inside the tent and saw he'd invited Gillian Morris, who lived two doors down from him. There was barely enough room for two, let alone the three of us. Gillian and I sat cross-legged facing Barry, our backs to the tent opening. Barry wasted no time.

"Show me yours," said Barry looking at me, "and I'll show you mine."

"I'll show you mine," piped up Gillian, who was a couple of years younger than Barry and me.

"I want to see Pauline's. Hers has hair on it."

I didn't remember this request being an encore. I shifted to my knees, pulled up my dress, and pulled down my knickers. Barry unbuttoned his trousers and pulled out his penis. Gillian and I gasped. The only penis I'd seen before then was my three-year-old brother Billy's when I had to give him a "top and tail" wash before bed. Billy's willie looked nothing like the one I was staring at.

"Do you want to touch it?" said Barry.

"No thank you," I said, as if he'd offered me a cucumber sandwich. I pulled up my knickers and backed out of the tent. Gillian was right behind me. We both ran home. Barry's curiosity must have been satisfied because he kept his trousers buttoned from then on.

Deeper in the park from where Barry and I built our cottage, was Lady Randle's orchard. I didn't know anyone who had ever seen the Lady, but we'd all heard the orchard's growling guard. Last year's memory would fade, and each autumn a gang of us would head for the orchard. The boys climbed the trees and tossed the apples to the ground, while we girls scrambled to gather the fruit, using our skirts as baskets. I thought it was great fun until I heard the distant barking. The boys tumbled down from the trees. We girls grasped the hems of our dresses with both hands to protect our bounty, and ran out of the orchard as fast as our legs could carry us.

Once over the wire fence we'd drop to our knees, laughing in fear. Our dresses, and the boys' short trousers, offered no protection against the stinging nettles clustered in the grass where we fell. We'd pluck the dock leaves growing beside the nettles, and rub nature's antidote on the painful bumps welling up on our bare limbs. I'd pick up my share of the dropped apples, and race home. I hoped Mother would make my favorite apple crumble with the stolen apples, and top it with steaming yellow Bird's Custard.

ELEVEN PLUS

After I walked the short distance home from Croyland Road Junior School, I'd peer out from behind the net curtains in our front bay window and watch Veronica Tapp and her friends pass by our front gate. The girls wore the green and gold uniforms of the Wellingborough Girls High School. Each had a brown leather satchel, bulging with homework, slung over the shoulder of her blazer, and a green bowler hat perched on her head. I wanted to be one of those girls.

Like the rest of the Country's eleven year olds, I was required to take the 11-plus examination. If I passed both parts of the exam, I would be able to attend Veronica's High School, where students were prepared for college. Failure meant I'd be relegated to a Secondary Modern School, where teachers taught the basics.

I was in my last year at Croyland Road Junior School when I took the 11-plus examination.

"You'll pass," several friends assured me.

I had mixed feelings. More than anything I wanted to attend The Wellingborough School for Girls, but at the same time, was fearful Mother wouldn't be able to afford the winter and summer uniform, satchel, books, and all the other things the high school required.

My friends were almost right. I passed the first part of the exam, but was rated "borderline" on the second part, which meant an oral interview was required to determine my final score. The interview was conducted in a large unfamiliar room. Several adults sat behind a long wooden table. I was directed to the first chair and asked several questions by the adult sitting opposite. I then moved to the next chair to answer questions from another adult, and so on, until I reached the last chair at the end of the table. One of the interviewers asked me to read a passage about volcanoes. I was a good reader, and had no problem with the assignment. After I finished, the adult asked me a question.

"What else has a core besides a volcano?"

My mind went blank—I couldn't answer the question. There may have been other questions I couldn't answer, or answered incorrectly, but that one looms large in my memory.

I didn't pass the oral examination. At the ripe old age of eleven, my fate was determined. My dream of attending The Wellingborough Grammar School for Girls was gone. I would be assigned to a secondary school. Unlike those who attended grammar schools, there were no expectations students finishing their four years at a Secondary school would aspire, or qualify, to attend college. At age fifteen I was destined to work in one of the town's boot and shoe factories, or behind a shop counter, if I were lucky.

I doubt many parents knew how wide the gap was between the two levels of education. I learned, years later, grammar schools received triple the funds per student than those who attended secondary modern Schools. We all knew the grammar school classes were more difficult, but who knew the teachers were better educated? Interesting, too, was the majority of students who attended grammar/high schools were from middle-class families, and those at secondary schools were from the working classes. Veronica Tapp, from our working class neighborhood, was an exception.

The history of the 11-plus examination process became even more interesting when I read Sir Cyril Burt, a well-respected psychologist, who was influential in the creation of the 11-plus examination after World War II, argued intelligence was predominately fixed by heredity. His findings were supported by some, and debunked by others. Ultimately, the 11-plus examination was mostly discarded in the 1960s, and replaced with a more egalitarian comprehensive system.

School wasn't just a place to learn. It was a place where I got a small bottle of milk to drink each day, and a healthy, and substantial dinner at noon. Each morning, when my teacher collected dinner money, she asked those children receiving free dinners to raise their hands. Two students raised their hands—I did, and a boy whose father had died. I was embarrassed and ashamed to raise my hand and have everyone in the class know I was too poor to pay for my dinner.

My shame was over by noon, and I gobbled up the main course of meat, potatoes, and vegetables, and sometimes had to restrain myself from licking the plate—which we all did at home. Some of the afters, though, were difficult for me to swallow. The steam puddings tasted like blobs of warm rubber—nothing like the mouth-watering rhubarb pies Mother made from the scarlet stalks she planted just outside the back door.

There was a valiant attempt to infuse some flavor into these steamed concoctions. Currents were impaled into one of the bland puddings and it became known as spotted dick. The dried fruit added nothing to the flavor in my opinion. Another attempt to make the pudding palatable was to pour Tate and Lyle's sticky, sickly-sweet treacle over the top. I managed to eat both of these versions, but I couldn't stomach puddings covered in red jam.

Students were expected to eat everything they were served. It was less than a decade after World War II, and memories of food shortages were still fresh. I managed to eat the plain pudding untouched by the jam, then I'd spread the rest around my plate to make it appear I had eaten almost everything. One particular dinnertime, Mrs. James, one of the most unpopular teachers in the school, sat at our dinner table. It happened to be a jam pudding day. Before I had a chance to flatten and distribute the jam-tainted pudding, she stopped me.

"Finish your pudding," she ordered.

"Please, Miss, I don't like jam," I said, and rose from my chair to leave the dining hall with the rest of my friends.

"Sit down and finish," she snapped.

I sat down. I looked at the lump of pudding on my plate and picked at a jam-free piece, then put my fork down. My table was close to the exit so all of the students in the hall filed passed me on their way out. Some of them smirked. I was so embarrassed it was easier to keep my eyes down, even if I had to look at the rotten pudding.

"We will stay here until you finish," said Mrs. James, and straightened her back even more.

The assembly hall had emptied, leaving just Mrs. James and me. I knew everyone would be talking about me, and all because of this stupid pudding. I had matured from my Infant School days to the point where I cared what people said about me. I couldn't believe what was happening. Nobody had ever forced me to eat anything.

But I knew one thing; I wasn't going to eat the pudding if my life depended on it. Mrs. James would have to sit on me and force it down my throat.

Mrs. James had afternoon classes to teach so I won this particular battle of wills.

I couldn't imagine Sandra Lambert, one of my best friends at Croyland Junior School, challenging Mrs. James as I did. Sandra was quiet and polite. She and I were opposites in looks as well as ways. I had wiry, black curls sitting on top of a brown face with big brown eyes. Sandra had pale cheeks dotted with freckles, light eyes, and hair twirled into red ringlets.

Sandra's mother, Mrs. Lambert, looked as if she'd stepped out of the page of *Women's Own* magazine. She was very pretty, with bright eyes, flawless skin, and hair the same shade of red as Sandra's, worn clipped back at each side with hairgrips. When she hurried, her spiral curls bounced on the shoulders of her fashionable frocks. Mrs. Lambert always wore bright red lipstick and looked like she was ready to go out—even when she was at home making tea. Sandra's father wore clean, pressed shirts and trousers with creases in the front. He was tall, with no unusual features, and jet-black hair slicked smoothly back from his face. I thought he looked like the film star, Cary Grant.

I never missed an opportunity to go to Sandra's house, which was in a housing estate on the other side of Croyland Park. Sandra was an only child at the time; a brother was to come much later. She and I were allowed to play in her bedroom, which was filled with matching white furniture, and billowy covers and pillows. With eight children crammed into our three-bedroom house, I never knew what it was like to sleep alone, much less have my own bedroom. For a time, my sisters Sheila,

Doris, Eileen, and I shared the same bed. Eileen wet the bed, and only after constant protests by the three dry kids did mother give Eileen her own bed.

Sandra and I spent hours on the floor of her bedroom playing with her Victorian dollhouse, and other treasures. When we tired of playing, we'd sneak into the sitting-room to spy on her parents. Crawling on our hands and knees through the open door, we'd peer around the side of the armchair, across from the couch where her parents sat kissing and cuddling. We'd spy on them as long as we could hold in our giggles, then clap our hands over our mouths and scamper back to the bedroom. Sandra's parents seemed to spend a lot of time on the couch. I was fascinated by their behavior. I'd never witnessed any affection between Mother and the Old Man.

Each morning, while I ate my cornflakes, often softened with hot tea because we'd run out of milk, my mother would warn me: "You come straight home from school. They just want you up there to amuse Sandra," she'd say. I didn't understand what she meant. I was happy at Sandra's house. I didn't even mind sitting on the cold step outside the house where she took piano lessons once a week.

I ignored Mother's instruction to come straight home and dashed off to Sandra's house after the four o'clock school bell rang. Although I knew I'd be punished, I decided having fun with my best friend was worth it. I often made these kinds of decisions. I'd weigh the consequences, then do what I wanted.

Mr. and Mrs. Lambert assumed Mother knew where I was, but there were no home telephones to confirm this. When it got dark early in the wintertime, Mr. Lambert would ask me if I had money to ride the bus back home.

"Yes," I'd lie, not wanting to admit I wasn't supposed

to be visiting.

Mr. Lambert would take my hand and walk with me to the bus stop. I'd look up at his handsome face as we strolled together—I wished he were my dad. At the bus stop I'd assure Mr. Lambert he could leave, anxious for him to go before the bus arrived. As soon as he was out of sight, I'd race down the gas-lit streets to the top entrance to Croyland Park. The park would be desolate, with barely a glimmer of light from the moon. The path through the park wound down a hill passed the big and little slides, the swings, and the roundabout. This area had no trees or bushes, so I wasn't afraid. Two sections always made my heart pound. Just beyond the swings was a short bridge where thick bushes had grown up on both sides of the brook which ran underneath the bridge—a perfect place for a bogeyman to leap out and grab me.

Once across the bridge, my final obstacle was the narrow entryway at the far end of the park leading to my street, where a grown man could hide in the shadows. At the top of the hill I'd take a big breath and run as fast as my short little legs would carry me. Down the hill I'd go, then sprint over the bridge—no bogeyman this night— take another deep breath to propel me along the final stretch up through the entryway to the safety of Mannock Road. I'd double over under the street light, and catch my breath. Now I had to face the music. I'd pray Mother had gone to bed and I'd be able to sneak in the house and not get a clout. I'd say the same prayer each time, and each time it was not answered.

I thought Sandra and I would continue to be best friends when we left Croyland Junior School and transferred to our senior school—John Lea Secondary Modern. I was devastated when, on the first day at senior school,

Sandra told me she didn't want to be my friend—she'd found a new one. I was the kind of kid who had one or two friends at a time, not a group of them. Sandra was my only friend at the school. I was in a new school with no friends.

John Lea School was just a few streets away from Sandra's house, so I walked to her home one day after school. I was in tears. I was sure a talk with Sandra's mother would make things better again—she would tell Sandra she had to be friends with me. I was still crying as I explained to Mrs. Lambert Sandra didn't want to be friends with me anymore. She looked at me with no expression on her face, and said, "Sandra is free to make her own friends."

I was confused, and hurt. I'd expected her to sympathize with me, and assure me she would talk to Sandra and tell her she had to be my friend again.

My hurt turned to anger. I did something I had never done before, and wouldn't dream of doing again. I spat on Mrs. Lambert's doorstep, then took one look at her stricken face, and took off like a hare. Mrs. Lambert never spoke to me again, and looked the other way when we passed on the street.

Fortunately, I wasn't rebuffed by anyone else, and was welcomed as a friend by three of the nicest girls at John Lea School: Jean, Joan and Christine.

STITCH IN TIME

Although I failed the 11-plus examination, I was consoled when placed in the "A" stream—the top class level—when I entered John Lea School. I was surprised and proud to be chosen as a prefect, a position of authority reserved for well-behaved students. My Croyland Road Infant School Headmistress, Miss Swan, would have dropped her jaw in astonishment at my transformation from a disobedient wild child, to an obedient and responsible student.

I wore my shield-shaped prefect's badge on the lapel of my school uniform blazer, and was vigilant about preventing my fellow students from running or sliding along the polished hallways.

John Lea Secondary Modern School had been open two years when I first attended in 1955. The school stood on 22 sprawling acres on the top of a hill above a cluster of council houses we referred to as the "new estate." Two driveways led to the school's main building. The driveway on the immediate left was for those who rode their bikes to school. Riders had to push their bikes up the narrow steep incline to park them. The wider driveway was the main path for the majority of students who walked to school, or for the few who arrived by bus from a neighboring village. School started at nine a.m., and if you arrived late, you would be marked in the "late book," by a student who waited at the top of each driveway. I dreaded being late—a concern not shared by my mother.

Occasionally, Mother would make me go to the post office before school to cash the weekly family allowance coupon. The Government provided all families with cash assistance for each child, beginning with the second one. This weekly allowance was often the only money keeping food on our table. No matter how much I cried and whined about being late for school, Mother pushed me out of the back door and told me to "Get cracking and don't forget to pick me up a packet of fags."

I'd run to the post office, which was three streets away, then wait in line to cash the coupon, purchase a packet of fags, run home, then dash out the door to school. I'd sprint the length of Croyland Park—over the bridge, passed the swings, and up the hill—then down the streets of the Kingsway housing estate. The keeper of the "late book" loomed large as I trudged up the final hill to the school.

The embarrassment of being late didn't damper my enthusiasm for school. After I took an exam, I'd anxiously rush to the back wall of the classroom where the test results were posted for all to see, and found my name at, or near, the top. English was a favorite subject and I excelled in reading.

Each morning before classes began, Mr. Wilce, the headmaster, would gather the school's students together in the assembly hall. After he made a speech from the stage, we'd sing hymns, and then recite the Lord's Prayer. There were mornings when I'd be waiting in the wings. Out of 600 students, I'd been chosen to read from the Gospel. My legs felt like ten-pound weights as I stepped slowly across the stage, carrying a Bible, to stand alone before the whole school.

"Fudge"

Standing on the school stage was less frightening to me, though, than standing on the edge of the open-air swimming pool at Wilby Lido.

The village of Wilby was a short bus ride from the school. Our class would arrive at the Lido in the early morning cold for swimming lessons in the unheated pool. As instructed, I'd line up along the concrete edge of the pool with the rest of the students—all turning various shades of blue. Our swimming instructor droned on about how to breathe bubbles in the water, oblivious to the chorus of chattering teeth—our bodies' involuntary effort to stave off the beginning stages of hypothermia. Then, the fully-clothed instructor would tell us to throw ourselves into the arctic waters where, "You will warm up once your shoulders are under the water." A theory the teacher had obviously not tested.

The rest of the girls and I seemed to have more trouble learning how to swim than the boys—a fact I attributed to the rubber caps we girls were forced to wear which were so tight they'd cut off all circulation above the eyebrows. I never learned how to swim while at school.

Not being able to swim didn't deter me from going to Wilby Lido in more suitable weather. In fact, most of the kids who lived in the vicinity of Wilby flocked to the Lido during the summer. Its opening in 1932 was announced with great fanfare by the local paper, the *Evening Telegraph*: "Wellingburians will shortly have within easy reach of their town, open air public baths fitted up on a luxurious scale..." –a slightly exaggerated description.

Our family couldn't afford summer holidays at Skegness, Blackpool, or any of the English seaside coastal resorts, so the village of Wilby became my vacation destination. If I was lucky, my friend Joy would bring me back a stick of pink and white rock candy from her holiday at Skegness. I'd risk losing my two front teeth when I took a bite, but it was sweet, and sticky, and fun to read the name of the seaside town embedded in a circle in the center, and visible down to the last bite.

Friends would also bring back from their holidays saucy seaside postcards created by the graphic artist, Donald McGill. These postcards often featured a large-breasted, scantily-clad young woman, and a randy guy, swapping double-entendres I pretended to understand. I would read years later that Mr. McGill's daughters were so embarrassed by their father's line of work he'd been quoted as saying, "They ran like stags whenever they passed a comic postcard shop."

Just once, Mother and a couple of us kids went on a one-day trip to the seaside—provided for free by the Old Man's employer. As I stepped off the bus, a blast of cold sea wind hit me in the face. I could smell fish. I'd looked forward to making a sandcastle like the ones I'd seen in pictures. There was no sand. The beach was nothing but pebbles, and when I took off my sandals to paddle in the sea, I quickly stumbled backwards out of the reach of the freezing cold water. I took my turn and sipped from the flask of warm tea Mother had brought along. After a couple of hours, we scrambled aboard a bus and came home.

Whether I loved school because I enjoyed learning, or whether it was a welcome escape from the chaos at home, I don't know. It may have been a bit of both. Some of the classes at John Lea were just for girls—such as Domestic Science, a fancy name for cooking and sewing—and some just for boys—such as woodwork and science. Physical Training, known as PT, was also taught separately. The boys played football, rugby and cricket, and the girls played netball, tennis, rounders, and field hockey. I loathed hockey. The weather was always rotten—cold and rainy—and when I played goalie, it was often for the winning team, which meant no action whatsoever. When I played a field position I was often whacked in the ankles with a hockey stick, which discouraged me from challenging the more aggressive players—not exactly a winning prescription.

Netball, a "girls" game similar to basketball, was more my style—lots of action. My friend Joy and I were on the school netball team. Our team actually placed top in our section one year. Joy was the team captain and played shooter, and I played help shooter—in my familiar place as second fiddle. When it came to sports, Joy was always ahead of me. I was convinced her superior athleticism grew from being the only girl in a family with four boys. The fact that she was taller, slimmer, with longer legs than mine, may also have worked in her favor.

I couldn't wait to start cooking class. I imagined sampling the scrumptious pies and cakes I'd bake. Our first class covered the art of washing, starching, and ironing our cooking aprons and caps. The next week's session focused on how to polish leather shoes with the reminder wet leather should never be dried directly in front of an open fire. To say I was disappointed would be an understatement. After what seemed an eternity, we began to make the pies and cakes I'd been looking forward to baking.

My culinary skills were on par with my classmates, until it came to baking bread. While all the other girls' bread swelled to a glorious soft mound, my dough turned into a rock. The teacher, whose sensitivity fell well short of her cooking skills, used my failed attempts as a lesson in how *not* to bake bread. This experience instilled in me a lifelong fear of any recipe requiring yeast.

There was one class which caused me more embarrassment than the cooking class—Miss Grey's music lessons. Miss Grey was a short, plump woman, who would threaten to bring in Mr. Jackson whenever she couldn't control her students—which was often.

Mr. Jackson was the most feared teacher at John Lea School. He wasn't much taller than Miss Grey, but he was stout, and he carried a heavy cane, which he whacked on the music teacher's desk—an action resulting in immediate silence. These were the days of corporal punishment, so the boys knew the next whack of the cane could very well be on their backsides.

As threatening as Mr. Jackson was, it was Miss Grey who caused me the most discomfort. As I entered her classroom, I would say a silent prayer Miss Grey would choose a different song. With the trillions of songs she could have chosen, she consistently chose the same one, "The Camptown Races." I'd sit at my desk facing the front of the classroom where Miss Grey sat at the piano banging out the tune, and instructing the class to sing along. Then we'd get to the verse with the word that made me cringe.

"...*I jumped upon a nigger 'cause I thought it was a hoss.*"

Each time, I would feel the heat rise to my cheeks. I was the one who wanted to jump—to jump up and run from the classroom—run all the way home. Instead, I would keep my emotions in check, and look straight ahead. Out of the corner of my eye I could see several boys sitting across the aisle looking over at me, and smirking. I'm certain Miss Grey had no idea her song selection caused me distress. She may not have known it was a minstrel song, written by the American, Stephen

Foster. When I found this out, I was thankful she didn't have the class perform the darn song in black-face.

Sewing class was part of the Domestic Science curriculum, designed to prepare girls for their eventual family duties. At our first class, the teacher asked each of us students to select a sewing pattern from those she'd spread out on tables on one side of the classroom. On another table were bolts of cloth, baskets of buttons, and other materials to complete the selected project. I chose a pinafore dress pattern, light green cotton material, thread, and a zip.

The teacher gave each of us a list of the material we'd selected and their cost. We were expected to reimburse her the next week. On the morning of my sewing class, I'd pleaded with my mother to give me at least some money so I could pay down my sewing debt. Mother would look at me as though I were crazy. "I don't have enough money to put food on the table, and you're asking me for money for a sewing class." I'd leave the house in tears.

Chalked in capital letters on the blackboard in the front of the class, were the names of students who hadn't paid the teacher for their sewing materials. My name was on the board, and it stayed there after all the other names had been erased. I dreaded walking into the sewing room, seeing my name on the board, and being beckoned to the front of the class by the teacher who wanted to know when I was going to pay her.

Janet was one of the students in my class. She was one of three tall, red-haired sisters who lived around the corner and down the street from our house. Jan and I were not what you'd call friends, but once in a while she'd turn the corner of my street at the same time I was unlatching our front gate, and the two of us would walk to school together.

Although Janet was only fourteen, she looked several years older. Rumor had it she was going out with American servicemen stationed at Chelveston, an air force base a few miles outside of town. It wasn't just her height which made Jan look mature, she was also reserved, and above tearing around the playground, shouting, and doubling up into fits of giggles like me and the rest of the girls our age. She ignored the shouts of the knobby-kneed boys in their short trousers as they rode by on their bikes, and the working men's wolf whistles through their lorry's open windows. Jan brushed aside these crude flirtations with the same nonchalance she flicked back her long, red hair. I wished I was as sophisticated.

Jan and I were walking home from school one afternoon when she took an unexpected turn onto an unfamiliar, quiet street. She told me we were going to her aunt's house. She unlatched the front gate and I followed her down the sloped pathway to the back of the house, and around the large black rain barrel to the back door. Jan stooped down and pulled out a key from underneath the horse-hair mat on the door step.

I followed Jan through the kitchen into the living room. There was a long, wooden mantelpiece, just like the one in our council house, above a fireplace piled with grey ashes from an earlier fire. The room was cluttered, but clean.

A curved, wooden china cabinet in one corner of the room caught my eye. Inside were delicate flowered porcelain cups and saucers, figurines, and several miniature brass pots sitting on glass shelves. Janet crossed the room to the cabinet, and turned the tiny key in the lock on the glass door. She reached into the cabinet, lifted out one of the brass pots, and tipped out a half-a-crown coin. "My Auntie Mary won't miss this one." I was shocked, but said nothing. I walked home with Janet several more times, and each time she helped herself to the silver coins stored in her aunt's china cabinet.

I didn't see Janet for a few days and heard she was ill. As I trudged home from school a day or two later, I turned the corner onto a quiet street. I unlatched the front garden gate, walked down the sloped path, and reached under the mat on the back door step. I entered the house, turned the key in the china cabinet, and lifted each lid on the three brass pots. I slipped three half-crowns into the pocket of my purple and grey school blazer with the prefect shield on the lapel. On the way back through the kitchen I sat down at the table, and helped myself to a bowl of corn flakes.

The next day I practically skipped into the sewing class. I reached into my blazer pocket, lifted out the half-crowns, and handed them to the sewing teacher. I stood and watched as she picked up the blackboard rubber, and slowly erased my name from the board. A week later, Jan caught up with me as I was leaving school.

"You'll never guess what happened," she said quietly. "Someone has been breaking into my aunt's house, and they took money from the china cabinet." Then she lowered her voice even more. "I knew it was someone besides me when my aunt told my dad that not only was all the money from the pots missing, but the burglar had the cheek to help himself to a bowl of cereal."

I kept walking, my head down. Then Janet said something, and my heart stopped.

"Can you believe all this went on and my Uncle Ted didn't hear a thing. He was working nights that week and was asleep upstairs."

I didn't say a word. I couldn't even look up at Janet. What if her Uncle Ted had woken up and walked downstairs? He might have called the police. They might have put me away. Friends and neighbors told me I was the best one in our family. I was a prefect at school. I never walked down that street again.

John Lea School was closed, and then demolished in 2001 despite "Save Our School," rallies led by Mr. Peter Bone, a local Member of Parliament. The stated reason for destroying the school was the lack of students, and the need for land for new housing. The irony is the additional housing brought more kids to the area and resulted in a school shortage.

A big "thank you" to Trevor Jones and Paul Ireland for developing and maintaining the johnleaschool.com website—preserving a visual record of John Lea School's history that otherwise would be lost.

John Lea School, Wellingborough

PART THREE
Loving and Losing

MATERIAL GIRL

I never confessed to anyone I'd stolen money from Janet's aunt. I didn't even tell Jean Minette, one of the three new friends I met when I began attending John Lea School in 1955 at the age of 11.

Jean's family had moved to our town from a city in the North of England, close to the Scottish border. They were a boisterous group, and even after short absences, Jean's family members would greet each other with the hardy hugs and kisses usually reserved for long-lost relatives. I was envious of the affection they showed each other. Mother and the Old Man never touched each other, at least not while they were standing up. Few of my friends' parents were as demonstrative as Jean's parents, so I decided it was because Jean's family was from the North. Since Jean's house was on my way to John Lea School, I'd stop by so we could walk together. Mr. Minette, a gangly, cheerful chap, would greet me with a "Where ye gwan?" I'd look at Jean for a translation. She'd hug her father, and tell him we were going off to school.

Jean was probably the prettiest girl in our school with her delicate features, clear skin, and short, thick, shiny, brown hair styled in what was called a "DA"—named after the shape of a duck's arse. I wished my hair was as easy to take care of as Jean's was. She just washed and brushed hers. I struggled to keep my "mop," as my mother called it, from looking like I just stuck my finger in an electrical socket. What a cruel trick fate played on me. I was dropped onto an island with an average humidity of ninety percent, and blessed with hair which, when released from rollers to smooth it, recoiled in protest the minute I stepped outside.

The boys at our school made no secret of their interest in Jean, and several of them would wait at the bottom of the school driveway, hoping for a chance to walk her home. Emboldened by their numbers, small groups of boys, who'd only recently traded short trousers for long ones, would break out with a chorus of, "I dream of Jeanie with the light brown hair," as she and I hurried by. Jean's cheeks would turn scarlet, which endeared her even more to the boys. I didn't get any comments—good or bad— which was okay with me.

One weekend, Jean's family invited me to go with them on a coach trip. These popular outings involved families boarding comfortable buses for a ride to somewhere, or other, with lots of stops at pubs. Choruses of "Knees up Mother Brown," would float out of the pub windows into the garden where Jean and I sat at a picnic table with the rest of the kids who were not old enough to go inside. Jean and I would talk, and laugh, and drink our bottles of orange pop, and hunt for the blue salt packet in our bag of Smith's crisps.

At one of the pub stops, Jean and I were sitting on a low stone wall swinging our legs, when a couple of young men strolled by. They chatted for a while, and asked if they could come and visit us the following week. With no shortage of suitors, Jean was hesitant, but I was all for it.

I was fourteen, and it was my first date. Mother made me a dress for the occasion. The material was bright yellow with a pattern of flowers and fruit. She didn't have a sewing machine and sewed the dress by hand, and without the guidance of a pattern. Mother never used implements to size or weigh, whether sewing, knitting, cooking or decorating. When she replaced the wallpaper in the living room, she measured by stretching her arms against the wall, rolled out the paper, slapped on some homemade flour and water glue, and then pasted the paper on the wall—matching the pattern—and all without an air bubble in sight.

I used most of my savings to buy my first pair of high-heel shoes to go with my new dress. The shoes were brown suede, which was not a practical material for footwear in soggy England, but, unlike leather, it would stretch to fit my wide feet. As I got ready to leave the house, my sister, Doris, who took a perverse pleasure in criticizing everything about me, broke into peals of laughter.

"You're wearing Mrs. Hadley's curtains," she shrieked with delight.

I rushed to look out of the back window and across the privet hedge at the neighbor's house. There, hanging in the Hadley's kitchen window, was my dress material. I resisted the urge to pull Doris' greasy brown hair out by the roots.

"Pay no attention to her," my mother soothed as I teetered out the door in my kitchen-curtain dress. My brown suede shoes were already killing me as they rubbed against my budding heel blisters.

Jean and I met the two young men at the top of Gilletts Road, up the hill from my house. They looked older than the first time we saw them, and what's more, they were Teddy Boys. The name "Teddy" came from the Edwardian-style clothing these boys wore. The outfit included a hip-length dark jacket with a velvet collar, very narrow trousers—known as drainpipes—and long pointy-toed shoes known as winkle-pickers—named after the pins used to take the edible winkle out of its shell. The typical hair style of the Teddy Boy was a scruffy imitation of Elvis, with extra grease on the side. Teddy Boys often congregated in gangs, and had a reputation for getting into fights. As nice girls, we were supposed to stay away from these blokes.

The only thing scary about the two boys we'd arranged to meet was their appearance. They were polite and treated us with respect. Jean and I held our date's hand as we strolled through the town sneaking a kiss or two. I did my best to hide the excruciating pain from the full-blown blisters on my heels, and was relieved when Jean said she had to get home.

Since the boys lived out of town, we found getting together difficult. My date and I wrote to each other promising to meet again, but we never did. The only letter he wrote began, "Dear Pet." I realized he'd forgotten my name, but remembered it started with a "P." I wasn't offended. In fact, I kept the letter for a long time. I never wore the yellow dress again.

Teddy Boys – circa 1950s

THE FANCY MAN

All of us eight kids were home from school. Mother was in the living room pressing her pink and white striped uniform, and starched white nurse's aide cap. She used the dinner table in the middle of the living room as a makeshift ironing board, with a thick wool blanket for a pad. The cord from the electric iron, attached to the plug in the ceiling light socket, swung back and forth.

The front garden gate crashed open against the wooden picket-fence railings. Timmy, our black mongrel, barked. Some of us kids scrambled to look out of the bay window. The Old Man was home. We never knew what mood he'd be in. One minute he'd be outside talking and laughing with the neighbors across the privet hedge, the next minute he'd be inside cursing and complaining in his strong Irish brogue.

The Old Man's sudden arrival made us all uneasy. He was never home before dark. The unease turned to fear when he came through the back doorway. I'd heard Mother use the words, "drunken bastard" before when even the bedclothes couldn't muffle the angry sounds from downstairs. This was the first time I'd heard them during the day.

The Old Man was wearing what he always wore— navy-blue railway overalls covered with soot, and a stained flat cap on his balding head. He lurched from the kitchen into the living room. In his hands was the sledgehammer we use to break coal lumps for the fire. He swung the hammer like a contestant in the Scottish Highland games I'd seen on television.

Tables and chairs splintered like matchsticks. The yellowed keys from the old piano shot around the room like missiles. Mother shouted for us kids to get out of the house. Crying and screaming, we pressed against the wall, and inched our way to the back door. After the Old Man smashed everything inside the house, he stumbled into the back garden. Headless birds and bloody feathers flew in every direction as he crushed his precious aviary. Then, either from exhaustion, or drink, he collapsed to the ground. Somehow Mother was able to sit on him, and keep him down until the police arrived. The Old Man wasn't arrested. He'd scared the life out of all of us, but it wasn't a crime.

It wasn't unusual for the Old Man to have irrational fits of anger. He would use his belt, or backhand any one of us for mild infractions, but I had never been as frightened of him as I was on that day. What had set him off? The following week we would all find out.

Mother was having an affair. I was eleven years old and knew what that was when I heard two neighbors talking at the bus stop. Our salacious Sunday newspaper, *The News of the World*, had provided me with that definition more than once.

I couldn't understand how Mother found the time or the energy for an affair. She'd recently been hired to work part-time at the Park Hospital. There were times when I'd come home from school in the afternoon and find her fast asleep, still dressed in her pink-striped uniform. Her head would be resting on a folded towel on the top of the heavy black iron fire guard.

We never knew how the Old Man discovered Mother's secret. After word got out, we heard whispers that Mother and her "fancy man" would meet in the grassy field across the street from the hospital where they both worked the night shift.

Following the Old Man's rampage, the atmosphere in the house became even more tense than usual. One evening, Mother served the Old Man a piping-hot plate of fish and chips. He took one look, and then flung the plate of food through the open kitchen door, and it landed with a crash on the cement path under the clothesline. He shouted out for Mother not to serve him anymore of her, "filthy English food." I wonder now what the neighbors must have thought. Here's this man, who epitomized every negative stereotype ever subscribed to the Irish— lazy, violent, alcoholic—disparaging the national dish of the country within earshot of his English neighbors.

Strange as it seem, there was a consolation to the frightening furniture-smashing episode.

Mother took pride in our home, and she longed for new living room furniture. The Old Man wouldn't hear of it. Mother purchased the furniture anyway, paying it off in weekly installments with the money she'd earned. The Old Man refused to have the old dilapidated furniture removed. So there we were, with two sets of furniture in a living room that was barely big enough for one set.

Mother's stylish Scandinavian sideboard and drop-leaf table were pushed up against the bulky, aged and chipped table, chairs, and piano that had occupied the room for years. Anyone entering from the kitchen had to climb over several pieces of furniture to reach the warmth of the fire on the far wall.

I don't know how much furniture was left after the rampage, but I missed the piano most. I would never again hear those mournful songs banged out by a steady stream of homesick, young Irish lodgers.

An ominous sequel occurred one afternoon about a week later. I heard Mother and my five-year-old sister, Delly, screaming as I opened the back door. I rushed into the living room. An electric plug dangled from a wall socket near the bay window. Mother was holding Delly, cradling her little arm that had turned black.

"It was meant for me," Mother yelled. She was convinced the Old Man had rewired the plug to electrocute her, and instead Delly had been the victim. Through some miracle my little sister suffered no permanent damage, but we all became more fearful, never knowing what would happen next.

"Someone had to go," Mother explained to us later. The Old Man refused to leave, so she went. She moved out of town with her fancy man, Sid Weekley. She deserted us—leaving eight kids with a ranting Irishman. Sheila, the eldest, was fifteen, Delly, the youngest, was five. I was eleven.

The Old Man's decision to stay and raise his brood, while mother led an unencumbered life with her lover, wore thin after a few months. One day, out of the blue, he announced, "The pack of ye can live with her."

He'd discovered Mother had moved to Market Harborough, a town about 15 miles away. We trouped upstairs and emptied the contents of our individual dresser drawer into cardboard boxes. Word got out among the neighbors all of us kids were being kicked out of the house. I trudged single file down the street with my brothers and sisters towards the bus stop. Some of us were crying. I could hear murmurs of sympathy from the neighbors who'd hurried to their front gates. "I'll take Pauline," I heard Mrs. Cox say as I passed by. She was a nice lady, but I didn't like her son and hoped I didn't end up at her house.

I was in the back of the group so I didn't see Mother's face when she opened the door and saw us all standing there. She let us in to a place with a bed and a stove in the same room. We crowded in, pushing and shoving each other.

"Can't ye see there isn't room for all of ye to live with me? You'll have to go back home," Mother said. Her words caused a hush in the tiny room. My older sister, Doris, was standing closest to Mother, crying and pleading with her to come home. I cried when I saw the others crying.

"I tried to get the Old Man to leave, but he wouldn't," Mother told us as she wept. "I had to go. He'd have killed me if I stayed."

We knew it could have happened. Before she left home, Mother's constant refrain had been, "Better the hell you know, than the hell you don't know." For too many years she was more afraid of the unknown than she was the cruel Old Man. She'd suffered enough.

We returned home to live with the Old Man. Without Mother the house didn't smell the same, and it never seemed to stay clean. I missed my mother in the way you'd miss someone who was once always there, but was now gone. But she and I had never hugged—never had any special moments together. I had always felt lonely, even when Mother was there.

The Old Man made salty porridge for us each morning, and the rest of the meals were bread and something. Many nights I'd be doing my homework when he'd come home drunk. Somehow the other kids managed to escape

"Fudge"

upstairs, and I was left alone with him.

The worst nights were when he'd turn on me. In case I'd forgotten—which I frequently did—he'd remind me of the color of my skin, and that I was illegitimate. This was the only time he singled me out for abuse.

When he leaned over the guard to spit in the fire, I'd dash out of the room. I'd still hear him ranting and raving about Mother—calling her every name under the sun—as I flew up the stairs. I fell asleep, thankful I was the little black bastard he'd called me. If I wasn't, then he'd be my real dad.

We had less money in the house without Mother's wages, and the Old Man continued to work when it suited him, which wasn't often, and spend what little he earned on booze. After Auntie Margaret died I never had anything new to wear. We all wore secondhand clothes and shoes—mostly hand-me-downs from within the family, or from neighbors. I was happy to wear cast offs from my friend, Dawn. The dresses she gave me looked almost new.

An epidemic of head lice flew through the house. We put newspapers on our laps and combed the fleas out with a small fine tooth comb. The eggs of the fleas were called nits and had to be scraped off each hair follicle with a finger nail. We must have looked like a bunch of monkeys picking through the heads of one another. It was the only time we touched each other without it being a slap.

With Mother gone, we must have looked so shabby that a neighbor, or a school teacher, alerted the Women's Royal Voluntary Service—a pioneer in social services. My brothers and sisters and I trudged to the grey stone WRVS building in town. A woman behind a high counter handed me a bundle of clothing and a pair of shoes. I was ashamed to be there, and felt poor for the first time.

I should have been more grateful. I was handed socks with no holes in the heels. I no longer needed to turn the sock heels around to the front so people behind me wouldn't see the holes as my secondhand shoes slid up and down. I should have been thankful for the new shoes I was given. They were the right size. I didn't need to wear two pairs of socks so they'd fit. I didn't need to cut out pieces of cardboard and slide them inside the shoes to cover the holes in the soles to stop my feet from getting wet from the perpetual rain.

And if it wasn't for the government's free noon-time school dinners, and the weekly family cash allowance, we'd have all gone to bed each night a lot hungrier.

After Mother left we had very few visitors. Neighbors, who once popped in to chat, stayed away—scared of the Old Man, just like we were. One evening, my younger brother Kevan and I were in the living room whispering to each other so the others wouldn't hear us. The Old Man was out drinking as usual.

"We could use those," I said, pointing to the large brass candlesticks on the mantelpiece.

"We could put them on top of the door." Kevan pointed to the door between the living room and the kitchen. We both grinned.

One of us said, "When he pushes the door all the way open they'll crash on his head and kill him." I'm hoping Kevan said it, but it could have been me.

"What if he doesn't die?" I asked. We knew what would happen to us. We dropped the plan.

The one visitor who did have the courage to visit was a stout, big-busted, redheaded Irish woman who Mother never liked. I didn't like her very much, either. The redhead would sit in our living room, in Mother's easy chair, with her knees wide apart. Fortunately she wore long dresses. She had a kid with her who was about three years old, and big for her age. The child climbed up and sat on her mother's ample lap and tapped on one breast. The redhead undid the safety pin which held together a flap cut out of her dress, and out flopped a large white tit. She proceeded to breastfeed this kid in front of the Old Man and us kids. If the redhead had designs on the Old Man, they were not reciprocated. At nighttime, she and her kid would end up squeezed into my double bed. The bed was already overcrowded with me, and two sisters—who were forced to sleep with their heads at the bottom of the bed, and their feet in my face, to make room for the uninvited guests.

About six months after Mother left, the Old Man came home drunk, yelling to the neighborhood as he came in the front gate, "I've killed the bastard."

I didn't know who "the bastard" was until I overheard him talking to his drinking friend, our neighbor Mr. Thompson, later the same evening. The two of them were sitting at our kitchen table. He was talking about Sid Weekley, Mother's fancy man.

"I watched the bastard get off the train," I heard the Old Man say. "He climbed on his bike. He didn't get far. I cracked him on the back of the head with a spanner." The details came out later. Sid had parked his bike at the Midland Road railway station where the Old Man worked. Someone must have identified Sid. The Old Man had chased him down the road, whacked him on the back of the head with a huge railroad spanner, and left him for dead. Sid was hospitalized, but survived the attack. This time when the police came, the Old Man did get arrested. He was sentenced to six months in Bedford jail. Everyone thought the sentence was light considering he almost killed a man. We heard the judge was lenient because he considered the attack a crime of passion.

My sister, Sheila, who was fifteen at the time, was the only one allowed to visit the Old Man in jail. She travelled by train to the town about 25 miles away. We were all ears when she'd come home.

"Do you know that prisoners eat everything with a spoon? They're not allowed to have a knife and fork."

We were shocked. I couldn't understand how they could cut their roast beef with a spoon.

"They also don't serve butter. They only have margarine." Shocked again. We knew the margarine part didn't go down well with the Old Man. He was used to the rich, tasty butter unidentified relatives sent from Ireland. I have no clear memory of how we managed while the Old Man was in prison and with Mother still away. The suffering of my younger sister, Eileen, who was about seven years old, was the most visible. Clumps of her hair fell out.

I only said prayers at school or in the Catholic Church, but one night I crept upstairs early so nobody would see me, knelt by my bed, and prayed Mother would come home. We heard she was waiting to see if the Old Man would get deported. If so, she would be safe. The Old Man wasn't deported, but he did return to Ireland to live after he was released from prison. He never came back to our house. He never said goodbye to any of us.

Harry Behan would die in Portlaoise, Ireland, in 1985, at the age of 80. I heard he survived by going from wake to wake where the drink flowed, and the food was free.

Mother came home. She'd been gone almost a year. Her return meant to me that God had answered my prayers, but only because, I reasoned, I didn't ask Him for anything very often. I resolved to bother Him only when it was very important.

Mother's home-coming must have been a quiet one. Nothing stands out. It was like when she left. One day she was there, and the next day she was gone. Then she was back.

Sid recovered and came to the house almost every evening. Sometimes Mother hid his shoes when he got ready to leave. Eventually he stayed.

I'm sure I wasn't the only one who thought Sid was nuts when he moved in with us. What man in his right mind would take on eight kids? We all thought the bang on the head from the Old Man must have loosened a few things.

Sid was about the same height as Mother, which made him shorter when she wore shoes. He was a little overweight—more stout than fat—and his brown hair was thinning on top. He wore glasses—apparently something he didn't need before he was beaten by the Old Man. I'd heard that Sid's bushy mustache concealed a cleft lip scar, a fact the Old Man jubilantly proclaimed during one of his tirades when Mother was gone.

Mother had a different life now. On most Friday nights, I could look out the front bay window and watch as she and Sid left the house, strolling to the pub hand-in-hand. Mother also had a different name. She was no longer Bette. Sid called her Liz. On the nights Mother didn't go to the pub with Sid, he'd return with a carton of Cadbury's Roses chocolates, Mother's favorite. How special our mother must have felt after all those years of being mistreated by the Old Man. Sid even climbed the stairs each morning to bring Mother a cup of tea in bed before he left for work.

One day I walked into the house and burst out laughing when I saw this short, stout, mustached, middle-aged man teetering around the living room in his wool socks and my mother's high-heel shoes. Mother, with the swollen corns on her little toes needed her new shoes stretched, and Sid obliged.

To see a man leave the house to go to work every day was something new for all of us—and it wasn't just Sid's work ethic that was different. The Old Man rarely changed out of his filthy railway overalls. Sid wore a suit and tie to his job as a bookkeeper in the office of Whitworths, a prestigious flour milling company located in town since the 1800s. Mother washed and ironed Sid's shirts, and starched the white collars. Sid polished his brown leather shoes 'til they shone. He secured the cuffs of his suit trousers with a metal clip, and every day, regardless of the weather, threw his leg over the cross-bar on his bike, and pedaled off to work.

Wellingborough was a small town, and it wasn't long before we kids found out Sid was married with a couple of kids—a son and a daughter. Someone pointed out Sid's wife to me as she strode by on the opposite side of the street near our house. She was tall, and straight-backed, and didn't seem to fit short Sid at all.

If Sid visited his kids, we never knew about it. There was one occasion when Sid crossed the street to the park to meet his son, who we'd heard was leaving to begin a career as a chef in another town. Mother was not happy about this meeting. She sat in her chair by the bay window with a sour expression on her face, chain smoking, until Sid returned. Mother even resented Sid's occasional visits to his Aunt Gert who lived just down the street from us, and who was so morbidly obese she rarely left her house. Sylve Evans, the barmaid at Sid's regular pub, was another target of Mother's insecurity—she made snide remarks about Sylve, convinced she was after Sid.

I don't know if Mother was pregnant when she returned home from Market Harborough, but it wasn't long after she began to show. I couldn't believe it. Mother was forty years old—too old to have a baby in my opinion. She already had eight kids and wasn't even married to Sid. When my friends came over I could see them staring at the bump under Mother's pinafore. I was 13 years old, and embarrassed.

I knew something was wrong when Mother had to go the hospital. She'd given birth to all the other children at home, as most people did. I heard something about a medical complication—about hemorrhaging. Mother came home from the hospital with the baby, a boy she'd named Malcolm George. She was still weak, and spent several more days in bed. Filled with self-righteousness, I refused to climb the stairs to see my mother and the baby.

Malcolm's eyes, like those of all newborns, didn't focus the first four weeks of his life. Weeks turned into months, and still the baby's eyes rolled from side to side. At four months, Mother had Malcolm fitted with glasses. She'd prop him up with pillows, in his pram, a pair of thick spectacles resting on his tiny nose. Mother would not, could not, accept that Malcolm had something seriously wrong with his eyes.

Six months after Malcolm's birth, Mother faced the devastating reality she had tried so hard to deny. Her sweet little blonde-haired boy had been born blind. He would never "...see the sun rise over Shannon, nor watch the sun go down in Galway Bay"—beautiful scenes from the Irish song she'd croon to him.

A BIRD IN THE HAND

I instigated the trip to London, and invited my friend, Judith, to go with me. I was fifteen-years-old, had completed my four years at John Lea School, and was working in a clothing factory, sewing bows on underwear and bored to tears.

In our house, once you turned fifteen and were out of school, you went to work and paid board. If any one of us complained about paying our way, as I did, Mother had an answer: "Don't let the door hit you in the arse on the way out."

Judith was actually a year or two older, but seemed younger. She was very shy, and her mother, Marion—"It's Judith, not Judy"—was very protective. I suspected Judith's shyness was the result of the curious looks people once gave her. Judith had a lazy eye when she was young, which required wearing a black patch over her good eye to strengthen the weak one. She developed a habit of walking with her head tilted to one side so she could see better. She continued to walk this way, even after the patch was removed, which made her look coy.

I'm not sure how our friendship developed because our personalities were not at all alike. I enjoyed a good laugh, and Judith looked embarrassed when she was having fun. Proximity may have played a role, since she lived on the same street.

"Fudge"

The only way to get to London was by train—a form of transportation I love to this day. Judith and I pooled our resources and took a taxi to Midland Road Station, an East Midland line since 1857, located on the outskirts of town. Ninety minutes later, after stopping in Bedford and Luton, the train pulled into Saint Pancras Station in the heart of London. Despite being two naïve country girls, Judith and I found it easy to get around London. Once we arrived at Saint Pancras, the adventure continued with a ride on the tube. These underground trains had color-coded maps stretched along the interior walls, with station names identified. We knew we wanted to go to Trafalgar Square with its famous statues, fountains, and flocks of pigeons—and arrived there without any problem.

The Square is a popular tourist attraction with an imposing column over 150 feet tall, topped by an 18-foot statue of Admiral Lord Nelson, Britain's famous naval hero. Judith and I had forgotten anything we were taught about the historic Battle of Trafalgar, other than it's where Lord Nelson was shot and killed. Our focus was on admiring the monument, and feeding the flocks of pigeons.

I wasn't a big fan of birds. I enjoyed watching them from a distance, but the flitting about made me nervous. My sister Sheila's pet budgie landed on my head once, and I can still recall those scratchy little claws digging into my scalp. I was determined to enjoy myself and not show Judith I was in the least bit nervous as the pigeons descended on me en-masse while a professional photographer took our picture.

We spent most of the day walking around the city. As evening approached the streets of London stayed as bright and busy as they did during the day. People passed us speaking with foreign accents we'd only heard in films. Mingling among the men in business suits and bowler hats were East Indians wearing turbans, accompanied by women with coats covering flowing silk dresses. Red double-decker buses lurched on the road close by us, and famous boxy black London taxis careened around pedestrian sightseers.

Judith and I craned our necks to see the tops of the huge, old, grey buildings towering above us. There were statues everywhere. I was thrilled to be in this great, noisy, city, so different from our small market town.

Somewhere along the way we met two Greek boys in their late teens. Their English was not very good, but we managed to communicate. We were having so much fun we forgot about the time, and not even a frenzied dash in a London taxi could get us to Saint Pancras Station in time. We missed the last train home. Judith and I had no idea what to do. We couldn't alert our parents, since nobody in our working-class neighborhood had a telephone in their house. The two young men talked to each other in Greek, and then offered to take us back to their boarding house.

"You'll have to be very quiet," one of them warned us, "because the landlady doesn't allow women in the rooms."

Judith and I looked sideways at each other. Saint Pancras Station did not look quite as inviting at night as it did when we arrived. We shrugged our shoulders and accepted the offer. As we climbed the stairs of the boarding house, Judith and I broke into a fit of giggles. The two young Greeks, ahead of us on the stairs, threw threatening backward glances, which only made us laugh even more. We clamped our hands over our mouths and stumbled up the stairs. I'm not sure what we were thinking, but it finally dawned on us we were expected to sleep with them.

We both stopped giggling and followed them into their separate rooms. The door closed and my Greek offered me some tea and bread. The bread was flat and tasted funny. It looked like my failed cooking-class bread the teacher used as an example of what happens when you kill the yeast. The Greek said he was tired, and we should go to bed. I agreed, but I wasn't going to take my clothes off. I was wearing one of my favorite dresses, a lavender silk shirtwaister. I'd purchased the dress from our neighbor, Mrs. Cook, who made a little commission selling items from a Littlewood's home shopping catalog. I still owed money on the dress.

After climbing into the bed, I scooted as far as possible to the other side, pressing myself against the wall. The young Greek climbed in behind me. I'd never slept with anyone but family members and didn't like it—and I liked this situation even less. The Greek kept breathing on my neck and putting his hands everywhere.

"I thought you said you were tired," I complained.

I was lucky he had the decency not to force the issue. I managed to get a little sleep, but would no doubt have slept more on a Saint Pancras railway station bench. The next morning I understood what was meant by the saying, "you looked like you slept in those clothes." I never knew just how wrinkled silk could get. I looked awful, and Judith didn't look much better.

Since the morning train home wasn't due for several

hours, we took the Greeks up on their invitation to visit the London Zoo in Regents Park—the oldest zoo in the world—an amazing fact that was wasted on me at the time. The four of us spent a pleasant couple of hours roaming around the zoo, and then headed to Saint Pancras for the ride home. Judith and I whispered throughout the train trip about our experiences of the night before. Judith had managed to fend off her Greek in bed, too. Neither of us realized at the time just how dangerous our decision to stay with two strange men had been.

With a houseful of kids to distract her, Mother didn't notice I was missing until breakfast. Judith's mother was frantic—she had only one other kid at home to worry about. Mother kept giving me dirty looks all day, and said it was my first, and my last trip to London.

No matter how hard I tried I could never get the wrinkles ironed out of my lavender silk dress.

ONE FRIDAY NIGHT

Swinging our stocking clad legs onto our bikes, our skirts hiked up, my friend Joy and I pedaled down London Road, taking turns overtaking each other, laughing as the interminable rain spattered our faces. It was Friday—pay day. The minute the whistle blew, we'd burst out of the doors of The Rubber Improvement, a two-story brick shoe factory, each clutching a small brown envelope containing our week's wages—a few pound notes and a couple of shillings.

Full pelt down Croyland Road we went, careening around the corner onto Henshaw Road, still laughing as we came to a stop at one of the identical brick council houses built close together in the circle of Henshaw and Mannock Roads.

"See you at seven," Joy shouted. "I'll come up to your house, so be ready."

Off I pedaled. Joy was such a bossy twit, although her reproach was based on her past experiences with me. I'd kept her waiting more than once. Just around the corner from Joy's house was the green garden gate at 84 Mannock Road. I propped my bike outside the back door and entered the tiny kitchen, surprised at the silence. *The Friday night card game must be starting late.* My brother-in law, Pete, would be heading across the street from his house soon, anxious to win a few shillings before we spent our week's wages. Mother stood by the kitchen sink, her pale, thin face drawn, her grey Irish eyes unsmiling.

"You need to pay your board before you go out," she ordered, holding her hand out.

"It's not fair," I snapped back. "Doris earns three times as much as me, and I have nothing left after I've paid." I resented the fact my sister, Doris, who worked at another factory earning more than most men, couldn't pay a bit more, and me a bit less. Mother did not subscribe to the sliding scale method of payment. In our house, once you left school at fifteen, you got a fulltime job, you paid your board, or you moved out. What little money I had left after paying board was eked out for entertainment, clothes, all toiletries, and even shoe polish. It was the same for everyone.

"You're the only one who complains," Mother said, taking two of the three pound notes I worked for all week.

I don't know why I continued to resent having to pay board. I knew what was expected. Sheila, the eldest in the family, who started working when I was still in school, had to pay up.

Despite having one arm, Sheila found a job soon after she left school. I was impressed when I learned she'd be a proofreader at Perkins the Printers. I expected to work in one of the dingy, windowless, boot and shoe factories after I left school.

Friday afternoon's Mother would send me downtown to Sheep Street, to wait across the road from the printing factory. Sheila, who'd been paid earlier in the day, would see me through the grimy factory window, then dash across the street to hand me her pay packet. She never complained. I should've been thankful I didn't have someone waiting outside my factory door to grab my pay packet.

"Fudge"

After I paid my board, I rushed by Mother, and headed upstairs. My mind was filled with the anticipation of the night ahead. "Tonight could be the night."

I now shared a bedroom with Doris and Eileen, two of my four sisters. Sheila had married Pete Sharp, and the youngest, Delly, slept in Mother's bed. An unused fireplace filled one corner, and a built-in wardrobe, blocked by one of the three beds, occupied another corner. A single dresser stood just inside the door, and each of us was assigned one drawer. I pulled open my sister Doris' drawer, thankful she'd left for the evening.

I was a little wider in the hips than Doris was, so her black slacks were tight, although not tight enough for me. I turned them inside out and stitched a temporary seam up each leg. I hoped the stiches would hold for one night. I rummaged through her drawer again to find a jumper which made my bust look bigger. Doris would throw a temper tantrum if she found out I'd borrowed her clothes. Once she threw her underskirt into the fire when she found out I'd worn it. I couldn't believe her reaction, and neither could Mother who told her, "You'd cut off your nose to spite your face."

All dressed up, I headed downstairs to wait for Joy.

"You'd better have your dinner before you leave," Mother called out. "There's fish and chips in the oven."

Along with pancakes on Shrove Tuesday, and hot cross buns before Easter, fish on Fridays was one of the few remnants of Mother's Irish Catholic upbringing.

"I'm not hungry," I replied. The excitement had taken away my appetite. Who would be there tonight?

"It's Joy," called out my little brother, Billy, opening the front door.

Joy and I had been friends for a long time, including our years at John Lea. We worked in one of the more than

20 factories manufacturing boots and shoes in Wellingborough in 1959. Jobs were plentiful, and the pay was good for those who could work fast. I wasn't one of those.

Joy worked in the factory office and operated a comptometer, having completed a month-long training course in Leicester, a large city about 50 miles north of Wellingborough. She complained how she had to bike to the train station in Midland Road in all weather, and then take the train to Leicester. I would have gladly continued with some kind of training, but was not given the opportunity. I was thrilled, therefore, when Joy helped me get a job in her office. Clerical work was considered more prestigious than working on the factory floor, although the pay was less. Mother thought I was nuts for leaving a factory job for one in the office. She was impressed with how much you earned, not what you did. Always the pragmatist, she often warned me, "Get your head outa that book. That's not gunna put bread on the table."

My "lofty" office position didn't last long. I was demoted back to the factory floor when the boss discovered I couldn't touch-type after all, and my hunting and pecking the work orders held up production.

I hated the dreary, monotonous, boring job on the factory floor making house slippers. I couldn't wait to fly out of the factory gate each evening.

Joy and I stayed friends even though we no longer worked together in the office. Mother liked Joy, referring to her as "Meggy" for some unknown reason. She enjoyed Joy's cocky attitude, and appreciated Joy trying to keep me in line. I didn't know the ages of Joy's parents, Mr. and Mrs. Robinson, but they both looked older than everyone else's mum and dad. Although he was a big man, Mr. Robinson had a soft voice, and never seemed to be in a hurry, unlike his bustling wife.

"Fudge"

For years, Mrs. Robinson volunteered her time as home help for housebound seniors. I'd wave when she rode by on her old, black bicycle with the basket in front. She biked for miles in all kinds of weather. I often wondered how her brown felt hat stayed on her head through the driving wind and rain. I realized how kind she was when she talked about her visits to the old age pensioners, some of whom, Mother joked, were younger than Mrs. Robinson.

Joy's parents were so thrilled when their fourth child was a girl that they named her "Joy"—a reflection of their happiness. I had a crush on John—Joy's second oldest brother. Many times, when I'd stop at the Robinson's house, a sleepy John would come stumbling into the living room, scratching his tangled blond curls. According to Joy, he was in perpetual recovery from nights at the pubs. He ignored me most of the time, but would sometimes mumble something in my direction. I wouldn't get it, but I'd laugh, anyway. I'd be embarrassed by the way I felt when I saw him, and thankful my dark skin, and the dim morning light, would conspire to hide the heat in my face.

Cars, and green double-decker buses, would whiz by as Joy and I linked arms and strolled up Gillets Road and turned onto Northampton Road, the main road to the county town of Northampton. We gabbed about the week at the factory, and the expectations of the night ahead, as we made our way to the Black Domino milk bar, our usual Friday night haunt.

On this particular night, as we sat in the café, Joy noticed me rummaging through my purse for coffee money.

"I'll treat you," she said. Joy always had more money than I did. I envied the fact that her parents didn't make her pay board.

The coffees were delicious, piping hot, frothy concoctions. I felt so cosmopolitan as I slid into one of the vinyl booths, coffee cup in one hand, and cigarette in the other. I had trouble sitting down in my tight slacks, and hoped the stitching would hold. Joy put her change into one of the miniature jukeboxes hanging on the wall.

"Cliff Richard," I'd plead.

Cliff was Britain's answer to Elvis. Another friend, Dawn, and I saw Cliff in person. We couldn't believe the way everyone outside the theater screamed when someone thought they spotted the rock star. Once inside we still looked down our noses at all this commotion. When Cliff sauntered onto the stage, the crowd exploded. Dawn and I looked at each other, and then let out bloodcurdling screams. For years we laughed about the silly moment.

Cliff's words came floating out of the jukebox:

"Got myself a cryin', talkin', sleepin',
walkin', livin' doll
Got to do my best to please her
just 'cos she's a livin' doll
Take a look at her hair, it's real If you don't believe what
  I say, just feel"

Well, Joy and I certainly thought we were livin' dolls, all dolled up for the night. I'm not sure about a couple of the lines though. Nobody could accuse us of having real hair. It was backcombed and sprayed solid—definitely not something a boy would want to touch.

"Pauline, do something with that wild hair," were the words I'd heard from my mother for years.

But what was it I was supposed to do? When I was a child I wanted my hair in plaits, like my sister Doris. Her hair was straight, easily brushed back and braided, lying flat on her head and touching her shoulders. My hair, curly in the back and frizzy in the front, was not easy to tame. Using a round hairbrush, with what I was convinced were nail bristles, my mother would rake my hair back from my forehead with one hand, and grip it at the nape of my neck with the other. I ended up with two thick pigtails sticking out by my shoulders. Clumps of frizzy hair in the front refused to lay flat. We couldn't afford the luxury of ribbons, so Mother would tie the ends of my plaits with sections of white bandages.

When I was old enough to do my own hair, I had an even bigger struggle. A visitor to our house on a Saturday morning would witness the same ritual. The kitchen windows would be steamed up from the saucepans of water I'd heated on the gas stove, since we had no running hot water. I'd pour some of the boiling water into the plastic bowl in the sink, cool it down with some cold water and dump my head in the bowl and start lathering my hair with the shampoo I'd purchased with the few shillings left from my factory pittance.

With my head bent forward full of soapy froth, I'd do my best to keep the stinging shampoo out of my eyes. Half blinded, I'd prepare another mix of boiling and cold water and scoop the warm water out of the bowl and over my head trying to rinse out the shampoo. I'd have no choice but to duck my head under the freezing cold tap water if I ran out of warm water before the shampoo rinsed out.

Sitting at the kitchen table with a small mirror propped up against the teapot, I combed out strands of hair and forced them around huge pink, spiked, plastic rollers held into place with hair grips. I didn't have a hair dryer, and I lived in a house which was almost as cold inside as it was outside, so drying my hair in time to go out at night was another challenge. I'd light the gas oven, kneel down on the red-tiled kitchen floor and stick my head as far inside as I dared with a head full of plastic. It's a wonder someone didn't call the police since, sadly, putting ones head in a gas oven was a popular way of committing suicide.

Using spiked hair rollers helped hold my hair in place while I curled it, but removing them required painful tugs. A couple of final steps were required to finish this production. I took the bottom two-thirds of my hair and pinned it back into a French roll. Then I pulled the top third up straight, backcombed it and smoothed it over into the popular Beehive style—aptly named because of the high conical shape. I'd spray copious amounts of hard-to-hold hair lacquer over the finished product. If I wrapped a scarf around my head at bedtime the beehive style would last for days. It was rumored insects could actually live undetected in these creations.

More than a few decades later I'd discover a book, "Curly Girl," by Lorraine Massey. I'd learn that curly hair should never be combed or brushed, and should be cut dry. That my hair should have been treated as softly as I treated woolen clothing—squeezed gently, never rubbed.

This Friday night, Joy and I were about to leave the Black Domino when a group of four blokes came into the cafe. They weren't local. They all had Elvis-style haircuts. Two of the boys sauntered over to talk to us. One seemed interested in me, and asked if I wanted to go outside to see his car. I was impressed. No one I knew owned a car as large and stylish as the baby blue Vauxhall Victor parked outside the cafe.

Ken Errington was his name, and he lived in Buckinghamshire, a county to the South. Ken became my first real boyfriend. I couldn't wait for him to call for me on Friday nights. I dreamed of having a steady boyfriend, and I didn't even mind that the name of his previous girlfriend was still tattooed on his arm. For the first time I felt normal. I had a boyfriend—someone special who liked me. I was relieved to no longer see the flash of pity across neighbors' faces when they'd ask my mother, "Is your Pauline courting yet?"—knowing full well I didn't have a boyfriend at the ripe old age of 15.

Before I met Ken, I was envious of the girls who had boyfriends. When the fair came to town and set up in Bassetts Close Park, I'd look wistfully at the couples screaming with delight on the rides—the girls with their frilly hoop skirts and their nice-looking boyfriends. I made an attempt to join the hoop skirt fashion. Mother couldn't afford the layered or hoop underskirt so I improvised by threading the hem of a standard underskirt with wire I found in the backyard. Unfortunately, the wire didn't have the flexibility of the shop-bought underwear. Early one Friday evening as a group of us girls piled onto the double-decker bus for the trip downtown to another popular café known as the "Moc," I sat down on the bus seat and my stiff wired underskirt caused the whole front of my dress to lift up revealing "my breakfast," as my mother would say. All of us screeched with laughter.

Ken joined the Friday night card game at our house and everyone liked him except my sister, Doris.

"He has really big knuckles," she'd said with a sneer.

This was hardly a grotesque flaw, but the remark managed to sting. Doris had a knack for pressing my buttons and I was too immature to cope. At twenty-one, six years my senior, Ken was no doubt too old for me, but

Mother liked him, although she wasn't pleased when he offered to buy me clothes. "It isn't respectable to take gifts like this at your age," she chided, displaying uncharacteristic propriety.

"If I didn't have to pay so much board I could buy my own clothes," I shot back.

I had the good sense to back away after the remark, and made sure I was in easy reach of the door handle. As I headed out the door, Mother took off her rubber-soled wool slipper and let it fly—missing my head by inches.

After a while, the difference in our ages, and the distance Ken had to drive, took its toll. One night, Ken told me he would not be taking me out any more. I was devastated. I telephoned him several times at his night job, crying, pleading with him to change his mind.

"Cry baby," Doris jeered when I returned from those crying jags in the red telephone box on the corner of Henshaw Road.

"I'll give you what you've been asking for," I sobbed to Ken one night. He was decent enough not to take me up on my desperate offer, and I, at last, accepted our courtship was over.

Cliff Richard—Britain's answer to Elvis

THE CRICKET QUEEN

I thought my sister, Doris, had an inflated view of herself, and this was confirmed when she competed for the title of "Cricket Queen," in a local beauty contest sponsored by the town's cricket team. To my amazement she was not eliminated during the first round. During phases of the contest, a taxi would pull up outside our house each Saturday morning, and Doris would emerge with an elaborate hairdo, and a new dress.

One Saturday, my mother and I peered out of the front bay window as a car pulled up to the curb. Doris made her usual royal exit from the taxi. Mother and I managed to stifle our laughter before Doris entered the front door. Doris' latest hairstyle was the most peculiar to date. It looked as if she were wearing an English cottage loaf of bread on her head. Her brown hair was gathered up to form two puffy rounds—the bottom layer billowed out like a well-risen loaf with the smaller layer perched on top.

Oblivious to our suffocated mirth, Doris was the happiest I'd ever seen her. She was usually in a sour mood, either constantly criticizing my appearance, or complaining about the food Mother prepared.

"Ham again," she'd whine if Mother served it two days in a row. She'd forgotten the days when all we'd have for tea was bread and dripping.

Doris invited me to go dress shopping with her. I was dumbfounded by the offer. As usual, I accepted the olive twig she offered. I watched as she tried on dress, after dress, in shop fitting rooms in preparation for the next stage of the Cricket Queen Competition. Although I thought my sister was plain, she did have a shapely figure, and looked quite attractive in some of the dresses, and I told her so.

To no one's surprise, except Doris', she was not crowned Cricket Queen, and had to be contented with being a Lady-in-Waiting to the chosen Queen. The next week, when I was dressed to go out for the evening, she came out with her usual remark, "You're not goin' out in *that*, are you?" she sneered. Her short period of good humor toward me was over.

Doris, upper left, with
Sylvia Biles

Wellingborough Parade-1959

MR. RIGHT

Doris' first, and only job, was working at The Mica, a sprawling brick factory in Wellingborough. She'd been working there a couple of years when I left my factory job at The Rubber Improvement, and also began working at The Mica. Doris became apoplectic. She'd always been ashamed I was her sister, and now I was working in *her* factory.

"With all the factories in Wellingborough, why did she have to pick mine?" she complained to our mother.

My new job was to splice small pieces of mica—shiny, thin flexible sheets of material used as electrical insulation—and size and classify them. Doris worked at the other end of the factory. I couldn't see her, but I could hear the sound of the noisy presses. Doris became the factory's fastest press operator, and made more money on piecework than any worker in the building.

Because of her speed, Doris was selected as the worker to be studied by Mr. Wright, a time-and-motion man who travelled to various mica factories around the country, to determine piecework rates. Mr. Wright, with his film-star good looks and immovable black hair, was the talk of the factory. Judging from the conversations I overheard, he stirred the fantasies of more than a few of the women. Wearing a crisp white coat and carrying a clip board, he'd stride by my bench each morning on his way to the press-operating section. Doris was seventeen years old when she was thrown together with Mr. Wright, who looked at least ten years older. They started going out. A rare opportunity had arisen to "get my own back" on my sister.

I couldn't wait to tell Mother I'd heard Mr. Wright was married. Doris had to know this too. One evening, Mr. Wright drove up to our house in his bubble car to take Doris out. Neighbors up and down the street heard my mother shout: "I'll turn that f--king car over with you in it if you ever come near her again."

Mother could have carried out her threat. Mr. Wright's bubble car resembled an aircraft cockpit on three wheels which Mother could have lifted with no trouble. My sister refused to stop seeing Mr. Wright, and made plans to move in with him. I was ecstatic. I would be rid of her at last.

Before Doris moved out, a visitor came to our house to see her—it was Mrs. Wright. I never understood handsome Mr. Wright's attraction to my plain sister with her mousy brown hair, thin lips, and a nose a little too long, although, unlike me, who was suffering with acne, she did have nice clear skin. I was more confused about Mr. Wright's interest in my sister when Mrs. Wright arrived. She was a stunning red-head with long shiny hair, perfectly proportioned facial features, and a nice figure.

Mother ushered me and the other kids into the kitchen, and left Doris and Mrs. Wright alone in the living room. With Mother in the backyard updating our neighbor, Mrs. Cook, over the hedge, I put my ear to the living room door and heard everything.

"He does this in every town he works in," the redhead told Doris. I admired how calm Mrs. Wright sounded. "He's not going to leave me," she added.

I heard my sister crying as she told Mrs. Wright, "We

love each other."

I was astounded Doris would say such a thing to the woman's face. I heard the front door slam. A week later Doris rented a flat in town and Mr. Wright moved in with her. In less than a month Mr. Wright went back to Mrs. Wright. The romance was over, and much to my dismay, Doris returned home.

The factory was ablaze with gossip. Everyone was talking about Doris' affair. They all knew Mr. Wright had returned to his wife. I was working at my factory bench the week after all this happened when one of Doris' friends came over to see me.

"Don't worry," she said sympathetically. "Doris is going to be all right."

I gave her a blank look—I had no idea what she was talking about. She explained my sister had been rushed to the hospital after collapsing at her press machine. Later I learned Doris had taken an unknown quantity of pills. She had her stomach pumped, and survived. I tried to conjure up some sympathy for Doris, but I felt nothing. I'd suffered years of her verbal abuse and I was numb. Her remarks about my teenage acne were particularly cruel.

"You put me off my food," she'd sneered across the dinner table one evening.

I'd been so tormented by remarks such as these, I'd scrubbed my face with a pumice stone 'til it bled. I was lucky I didn't leave permanent scars.

Following Doris' suicide attempt her skin broke out in blemishes and looked worse than mine ever did. She never recovered her previously flawless complexion. My acne eventually cleared up.

BMW British-registered LHD 3-wheeled Bubble Car, similar to the one that Mother threatened to overturn—circa 1950s

PART FOUR

Beginnings and Endings

FRANK THE YANK

I thought Frank was a bit odd when I first met him, but I put it down to his being an American. I told myself his behavior was just a cultural thing, something to be understood, like his Virginia accent. A year before I met Frank I'd been rejected by my English boyfriend, Ken Errington, and at sixteen, having a boyfriend, almost any boyfriend, was more important to me than having the right boyfriend.

Chelveston, the local American air force base where Frank was stationed, was a magnet for girls living in the surrounding towns and villages. Friday and Saturday nights, groups of young women would pool some of their weekly wages to pay for a taxi ride to the Base. The servicemen at Chelveston were as popular with the local girls as the World War II soldiers had been with many of the girls' mothers—and for the same reasons. The Americans talked like Hollywood film stars, smelled nice, and were very generous.

Frank shared the barracks with Jim Parker, a young airman I'd been dancing with at The Club, as it was known. Jim was a quiet, respectful young man. He was so polite he asked permission before we kissed the first time. I arrived at The Club one night, and Frank introduced himself, and told me Jim was on night duty. Frank borrowed his friend's sports coat to meet the Airmen's

Club dress code, and later the same evening, borrowed me, Jim's girlfriend. The Americans referred to this sport of stealing their buddy's girlfriends as "shooting him out of the saddle."

I didn't see Jim at The Club after Frank and I met, so I continued to date Frank.

I'd heard of Chelveston Air Force Base long before I attended dances there. As usual, my information came from eavesdropping on conversations between my mother and her friends, who often reminisced about the war years. Apparently, Mother drove a tractor on the base when it was being prepared for the incoming American Eighth Air Force. I wondered if my father had been stationed there, but I never asked my mother.

The dances I attended at The Club were in stark contrast to those at our town's Working Men's Club. There, most of us girls stood around tapping our toes to blaring gramophone records, and ended up dancing with each other. The boys were comfortable with this arrangement until just before the last dance, when they'd make a mad dash for a girl, and hoped they'd earned enough credits for a little "slap and tickle" on the walk home.

In contrast, the American club had a live band, round cloth-covered tables encircling a wooden dance floor, and soft lighting. The American airmen danced all night, and looked as if they enjoyed themselves.

Frank and I started courting. He didn't have a car, and there was no bus service from the base to my hometown, so I was flattered he hitchhiked to see me as often as he did. He was nice looking, and a generous and attentive boyfriend, but he still managed to get on my nerves. I was appalled at how tactless he could be. He would criticize all things English, claiming everything was made in America and, what's more, "made much better." He also

"Fudge"

saw it as his duty to teach me how to pronounce certain words.

"Nestles chocolate is American," he'd announce, "and it's pronounced "Neslees" not "Nessels." He also said I pronounced aluminium incorrectly. "There are four syllables, a-lum-in-um," he'd declare, and "Woolworth's is also American," he bragged one afternoon when we strolled passed the popular shop in the town center on Market Street.

Not content with lecturing me on the origins of international corporations, and American pronunciation, Frank had an opinion on construction. "You people don't know how to build houses," he'd say loud enough for the carpenters to hear him as we strolled passed a house under construction. "You don't use any insulation either."

He might have been right about the origins of the international corporations, and I knew nothing about insulation—but I knew it was ill-mannered to brag and criticize when you were the guest of a country. He even told me a crude "joke" when he found out my mother had nine children.

"I like cigars too," he said, "but I take them out of my mouth once in a while." As usual he cracked up at his own joke. Frank's remarks were becoming more and more annoying to me, but I was flattered by the attention and gifts which gave my damaged ego a boost. On Valentine's Day, he hitchhiked to my house carrying the largest heart-shaped box of chocolates anyone in the vicinity had ever seen. Doris couldn't disguise her envy.

Frank and I never discussed race, which didn't seem odd to me then, but does now. There was one incident. A G.I., who was dating a girl who lived on our street, spread it around the base I was half-black. I was surprised this was newsworthy since it was obvious to anyone who could see. Frank was so outraged he wrote the name of the G.I.'s girlfriend on the men's military bathroom, along with some choice words, no doubt. He thought this, too, was hilarious.

My sister, Doris, couldn't stand Frank, of course, since he was my boyfriend. He was delighted to retaliate against her, which may have been another reason I continued to date him. I had someone to defend me against the onslaught of Doris' criticisms and insults.

Doris had the nasty habit of sniffing whenever she passed me in the house. It had the desired effect of upsetting me. Frank would give a huge sniff whenever he walked by Doris, which upset her enough to make her leave the room. I was too immature to understand Frank's behavior toward my sister, although appreciated by me at the time; it revealed yet another flaw in his character.

I was glad to have someone side with me against Doris, but it wasn't enough. I told Frank I didn't want to see him anymore. This took courage on my part because he was my first sexual partner, and I didn't see myself as someone who had sex with someone with whom I wasn't seriously considering marriage.

Frank ignored me, and kept showing up at my house. When I became adamant about breaking up, he informed me he'd notify the Base authorities I was underage. I was almost 17, but the minimum age to enter The Club was 18. My dancing weekends at the Base would be over. If I'd been more secure, I would've told Frank where to go, but all I could think of was I'd be alone again—spending my Friday and Saturday nights sitting by the coal fire smoking Senior Service cigarettes. I continued to go out with him.

I realized too late I should have listened closer to Mother's obscure birth control advice: "Keep your hand on your ha'penny 'till you get your toffee."

Well, the ha'penny got spent after a few too many Singapore Gin Slings at The Club, and after-dark walks in Croyland Park. I found out I was pregnant during the time Chelveston Air Base was closing down, and all American personnel were being shipped to Toul Rosiers in northeastern France.

"We'll get married," Frank announced.

I wasn't thrilled with the idea of marrying him, but was a lot less thrilled about being an unwed mother, a condition fast becoming an epidemic in our small town. To demonstrate he was serious, Frank gave me an engagement ring with a single diamond in the shape of a heart. I removed the ring whenever I put my hands in water, and one day it slipped from the soapy ledge above the sink, and was flushed down the drain. I should have taken this as an omen.

Airmen contemplating marriage to a foreign national were required to meet with the base chaplain. Frank was eighteen years old, and too young to marry without parental consent, so our meeting with the chaplain doubled as a counseling session and a report for his mother, who was divorced from his father and living in Roanoke, Virginia.

When Frank came to see me a few weeks after our counseling session, he was furious. His mother, Alzona, had refused to sign the marriage consent form. She told Frank that the chaplain said I appeared to be of mixed-race. I now knew I hadn't imagined the severe look the chaplain gave me when I entered his office.

Frank telephoned his mother and I listened as he berated her for not giving permission for us to marry. I was flabbergasted he would talk to his mother this way, and knew he was only alienating her even more. This whole melodrama delighted Doris. She now had even more ammunition for her spiteful remarks. For most of my life friends and neighbors would smile and assure me I was, "...the best one in the family." I can only guess this description was based on the fact that I did well in school, and had never been in trouble—or at least not been caught. I also didn't use the local slang—some called it "speaking posh"—and I didn't swear.

"Who do you think you are, Lady Muck?" was one of Doris' frequent taunts.

Well, not anymore. I was in the "pudding club" and soon everyone would know it.

One afternoon my brother, Terry, told me he'd seen Ken, my ex-boyfriend, in one of the neighboring villages and Ken had asked how I was doing. The next week Ken knocked on my door. Ignoring my mother's objections, I climbed into his baby blue Vauxhall Victor, and we went for a ride. I cried as I told him I was pregnant. He had come back too late.

Frank left for France with the rest of his squadron. He kept his promise and wrote to me, and sent as much money as he could afford. I sat home knitting baby clothes, and inflating like a beach ball. In my letters to France I shared how miserable I was. Doris was getting nastier now she had my pregnancy for extra ammunition. Frank continued to ask his mother for permission to marry. She wouldn't budge. Before he left for France, we investigated going to Gretna Green, in Scotland, where you could marry without parental consent if you were at least sixteen. Unfortunately, we couldn't meet the 15-day residency requirement, and Frank's American citizenship might have also been an impediment.

Although Frank didn't get promoted on par with other airmen, he managed to save enough money to pay my fare to France. I survived a rough ferry crossing over the English Channel where I joined most of the passengers below deck, being seasick. After I disembarked, I became frantic when I discovered I'd arrived at the wrong French port, and had no clue why. I had no way to contact Frank, and no money for a return trip home.

I wandered around the port scared, tired and miserable. As I crossed a short bridge I looked down at the black water and thought about jumping in. I knew my heavy suitcase would take me to the bottom. The thought passed quickly. I was tired and hungry and on the verge of collapse. I trudged along until I found a café where I could sit. My pregnancy was obvious now. An elderly Frenchman got up from his table and came over to mine. He spoke English and offered to buy me something to eat and drink. I was more hungry than wary, so I accepted his kind offer. He sat with me for a short time, and then left.

Two port gendarmes approached me as I sat alone in the café. They asked me for identification and wanted to know where I was going. Since I didn't have any money I was considered a vagrant under French law. The gendarmes escorted me on to the ferry and shipped me back across the Channel. The British police met me on the other side and brought me home. They reminded my mother a bill for transportation would follow.

My next excursion across the English Channel a few weeks later was more successful. I spent several months in Toul Rosiers travelling around villages with Frank, hoping a French priest would marry us—none would because we were both foreigners. I returned to England, alone, in my ninth month of pregnancy.

After another rough Channel crossing, I awoke early the next morning at my mother's house and waddled down the stairs toward the outside toilet. I was mortified because I was peeing as I descended the stairs. I called out for my mother.

"Your water broke," she said. I was scared and started to cry. "You'll be alright," she said gently.

I gave birth to a beautiful baby boy in the Wellingborough Park Hospital where Mother once worked. All the nurses said he was lovely. I named him Dean.

What a luxury it was to recuperate for ten days in the hospital and get some sleep while the nurses tended to the baby during the night. Mother visited and brought my favorite apple crumble and custard.

I think back now to when I was 13 years old, and so ashamed that Mother had her baby Malcolm out of wedlock that I wouldn't walk up the stairs of our house to see either of them.

The day before I was due to be discharged from the hospital I was holding my baby boy in my arms, gazing at his sweet face, when I overhead one of the nurses aide's whisper something to the mother in the bed next to me, "She isn't married."

I was stunned. I knew she was talking about me. A tear escaped from each eye and slid down my cheeks. I knew if I told Mother, she would have kicked the aide's arse.

The hospital rules were strict, except, apparently, when it came to patient confidentiality. One morning I'd washed my hair and put in enormous pink rollers. As one of the nurses made her morning rounds she approached my bed. "Get those rollers out," she demanded. "Matron will be here in a few minutes."

I didn't argue, and pulled them out just before Matron, in her distinctive blue dress, white collar and cuffs, and huge starched cap, entered the ward. I sat straight up in bed and almost saluted.

"Fudge"

On my way home from the hospital I stopped at my sister Sheila's house in the Kingsway Estate where she had recently moved. Sheila had a surprise for me. On the same day I delivered my baby, Sheila had been taken to Kettering hospital, in another town, and given birth, prematurely, to her second child, a boy she named Richard.

The living arrangements at Mother's house were not ideal. There were eight kids still living at home. The bedrooms were so cold I slept on the couch downstairs next to the fire with my baby son next to me.

I'm sure I was even more of an embarrassment to Doris as an unmarried mother, although her feelings toward me were not extended to my son.

"Whenever you leave the house, Doris scoops the baby up from the pram and coos to him before you've reached the front gate," my mother told me, as she and I sipped tea alone in the kitchen.

One evening, I awoke to the faint sound of baby Dean coughing. I was terrified to see he was choking and turning blue. I screamed for my mother, and she and Sid rushed downstairs. Mother sent me to fetch a nurse who lived nearby, and I slid and slipped my way in the snow, up the hill to her house. While I was gone Mother and Sid managed to breathe life back into my baby.

Dean often spat up after finishing his bottle. It happened so often Mother nicknamed him "spooie." I thought the baby spat up because he drank too much, too fast. I'd tried to breastfeed him, but with a houseful of curious kids, and only one warm room, it was too difficult. Dean may have actually been allergic to the milk I gave him, but people rarely thought about allergies in those days. I slept fitfully for many nights. I was afraid Dean would roll over onto his back again, spit up, and choke himself to death.

Frank's assignment at Toul-Rosieres was a short one. French President, Charles de Gaulle, while remaining a member of the North Atlantic Treaty Association (NATO), was withdrawing from the NATO military command citing the need for French independence in world affairs. He ordered all foreign troops out of France—which included the Americans. Fifty years later France would rejoin the NATO military command.

Frank was granted a humanitarian re-assignment to England to be with me and the baby. He was stationed at RAF Alconbury when he got the news his mother had relented. She gave her permission for us to marry. I'd sent her a photograph of the baby and perhaps this had swayed her. Frank and I were married at the Wellingborough Registry Office with Mother and my friend, Dawn, in attendance. Dawn and I giggled throughout the ceremony—at what, I have no idea.

The four of us went to the studio of the photographer, Rex K. Davis, in Oxford Street, to record the occasion. I was 18 and Frank was 19. I was relieved to be married. I felt respectable again. Frank displayed some personality quirks during our courtship but he was loyal, and he accepted responsibility for fathering my child. When he was transferred to France he had the perfect opportunity to ditch me, but he didn't. I suspected his decision to stick by me included a determination not to let either his mother, or my sister, Doris, have the upper hand.

When we returned to Mother's house from the studio I was surprised to see people had gathered for a small wedding reception. Later I learned from Mother, that Doris had arranged the party, and purchased, and prepared the refreshments. Doris was the last person I thought would ever do anything nice for me, given how hatefully she'd always treated me. I don't think I thanked her.

At the time I was living at home with my baby, Mother was coping with five-year-old Malcolm. In addition to the challenges his blindness presented, Malcolm was having seizures. He'd fly into rages, stumbling around the living room throwing everything he could get his hands on. I had to make sure my baby was protected at all times, and everyone in the house learned to duck.

Malcolm's blindness prevented him from running around like most kids his age, so he had loads of pent-up energy. Mother didn't want him playing with the kids in the neighborhood. She was cynical by nature, and didn't trust them.

"He's not gunna be gawked at," she would say. He wasn't going to be a curiosity if she could help it. Sid, Malcolm's dad, wanted his son to lead as normal a life as possible, and managed to talk Mother into letting the next door neighbor's boy into the back yard so the two could play football.

I watched Sid as he lifted the corrugated metal roof off the chicken run in the back yard and propped it against the privet hedge which separated our yard from our next door neighbors, the Cook family. Sid told Malcolm he was the goalie and led him across the yard where he stationed him in front of the metal sheet. The neighbor boy stood a few yards from Malcolm and kicked the ball toward him. The object of the game was for the neighbor kid to get the ball passed Malcolm. He helped out by shouting, "Go right," or "Go left" so Malcolm could stop the ball. Most of the time Malcolm didn't save a goal, because neither little kid knew their right side from their left. But between his friend's directions, and the sound of the ball ricocheting off the metal roof, Malcolm could at least locate the ball and throw it back. Malcom laughed and jumped up and down, flicking both wrists simultaneously—something he often did to expend energy.

The doctors urged Mother to place Malcolm in the Sunshine Home for the Blind—a boarding school in the next county. He would learn Braille, they told her, and be around other blind children. The Home was once an historic private estate, and it sat on acres of land. None of us could imagine Mother agreeing to part with a five-year-old child. We also knew how she felt about boarding schools.

When Mother was living with the Old Man, she'd worked part-time as a housekeeper at the prestigious Wellingborough Public School—a private facility. She'd told us Dickensian tales of boys as young as five being caned for wetting the bed, then being forced to wash their bed clothes in freezing cold water. These were not her only criticisms.

"Some of these kids had parents who were rich foreigners, and they'd feed these kids food I wouldn't give to a dog."

Sid talked Mother into taking a tour of the Sunshine Home.

"Staff at the school is lovely to the children," she told us when she returned. She marveled at how much the children could do despite their disabilities.

"They can dress themselves and tie their own shoes," she'd reported. Mother wouldn't let Malcolm do anything for himself. "It's lovely to see," she told us after another one of her visits. "They're so worried about the kids' safety they have signs posted around the town telling motorists to watch for blind pedestrians."

When Mother and I were alone, she mentioned an

incident which occurred at the Home.

"There are some colored children in the Home," she said. "None of the other blind children would know the difference, but the staff calls out to them—identifying them as colored."

Mother and I looked at each other—each sharing the same thought. Even among the blind, the non-white children were singled out, and made to feel different.

Although Mother's reports about the school were mostly positive, she couldn't keep the anguish from her voice when she told us she'd agreed to let Malcolm go. I, for one, was relieved. Mother's misguided over-protection and doting had turned Malcolm into an incorrigible little brat. In addition to lobbing missiles, if anyone was watching television and Malcolm wanted it turned off because he couldn't see what we were laughing at—off it would go. I felt sad for Mother, but even she must have felt some relief at the prospect of getting Malcolm domesticated.

(L-R) Mother, Frank, me and Dawn
Wedding Photograph
Wellingborough,
March 1963

WILBY LIDO

If I thought being married to an American would mean an upgrade in my living quarters from my mother's council house in Mannock Road, I was mistaken.

My husband's inability to get along with his supervisors meant he was passed over for promotions. Frank had two stripes, one less than most airmen with his seniority, and while his pay was plenty for a single soldier, it wasn't a lot for a married man with a baby.

Frank was resourceful and managed to find us an inexpensive caravan to rent in the Lido, in Wilby—a village a short distance from Mother's house. It wasn't much, but it was a place of our own. I couldn't have imagined six years after those unforgettable swimming lessons at John Lea School, I'd end up living at Wilby Lido—although it wasn't a lido anymore. The pool and snack bar had closed four years earlier, after twenty-five years in operation. It was now a permanent caravan home park.

The caravan Frank rented was designed for a week by the seaside—not for permanent living. The interior was so narrow one of us had to scoot onto the two-person eating booth to let the other pass. There was no water connected to the caravan, so each morning I'd brave the freezing cold and lug a bucket to the communal tap. I'd cook, heat water, and sterilize the nappies of my four-month-old son on the miniature gas stove.

We stayed at the Lido the winter of 1962/63 which was recorded as one of the most bitterly cold on record, and was dubbed "The Big Freeze." Newspapers reported the snow in some parts of England "...was as deep as the hedgerows were high! People managed to walk on the tops of the frozen shrubbery, rather than risk driving through the deep snow." Snow was so deep in parts of England that newspapers pictured milkmen delivering milk on snow skis.

The cramped eating area in the caravan converted to a bedroom at night. Frank and I went to sleep staring at the embers of the coke fire, two feet from our fold-out bed, but at least we, and the baby, were warm.

It would take several months after we married before we received the air force housing allowance. So we wouldn't starve in the meantime, Mother prepared hot dinners and had my twelve-year-old brother, Billy, perform a "meals on wheels" service. Billy pedaled his bike uphill the three-miles to Wilby Lido, and managed to deliver the meals to us intact.

Billy had enough strength left after his journey to hoist up my hefty baby for a quick photograph.

I didn't complain about my living conditions. I was content to have a quiet place I could call my own with nobody to aggravate me. As soon as Frank received the housing allowance we moved from the Lido to Burton Latimer, a small town five miles from Mother's house. I was 18 and pregnant with my second child.

Our married life was a continuation of our courtship.

"Fudge"

Frank didn't get any more sensitive, and his temper became easier and easier to arouse. He thought nothing of giving me a slap across the face if he was losing an argument. I had a quick tongue and wasn't afraid to speak my mind, even when it would have been prudent to wait 'till things calmed down.

The first time Frank slapped me should have been the last. But I'd grown up with violence. That's how the Old Man and Mother vented their frustrations. That's how my brothers and sisters and I vented ours.

The sparsely furnished two-bedroom house we rented in Burton Latimer was one of five nineteenth century terrace row houses on Finedon Street. There was no front garden. Passers-by could look straight in the front window from the street. Each of the five houses had small backyards separated by a waist-high fence. To enter my back door, I had to walk through the back gardens of the other four houses.

A private party owned the houses, and four of the five were rented to families of American servicemen at, I'd guess, an inflated rate. Three of the American airmen were married to British girls, which included me, and one to an American girl. Carol Cobb was the American wife, and she'd host morning coffee for the rest of us.

Carol, and her husband Russell, were from Massachusetts. They had two pre-school daughters—Robin, blond and precocious, and Donna, brown-haired and quiet. Carol was the only one with a washing machine—a monstrous, noisy American contraption with a wringer attached to an agitator tub. Terry and Mary, the two British wives, and I, each had a baby under the age of two, so we were delighted to take Carol up on her offer to join the communal washing day at her house.

In December 1963, one month after the devastating

assassination of President Kennedy, I gave birth to a beautiful baby girl at the Park Hospital where I'd delivered my first baby 13 months earlier. We named her Tina. I was now a "respectable married woman," and wasn't subjected to the hurtful gossip I'd overheard during my first delivery.

I'd read where some mixed-race children fretted about how dark or light-skinned their offspring would be. I assumed my babies would be just like everyone else's children—a mix of both parents. This didn't happen with Dean and Tina. Both had coloring more like their father's than like mine. Each had very light skin and brown hair. Tina's hair was straight for most of her life, and Dean's was wavy. I wasn't sorry the children didn't look more like me. They'd have challenges like all children, but not the racial bullying that was inflicted on me.

Most mornings I'd bundle up my two babies and meet with the other mothers in my neighbor Carol's kitchen. We'd have candid conversations about our husbands, but never talked about the racial problems in America—at least not while I was around. Racial, and other discrimination, wasn't illegal in the United States at the time. The Civil Rights Act, banning such practices, would not be enacted until a year later.

After Carol and her husband were transferred back to the U.S., Mary, one of the British women, told me Carol was concerned about how I might be treated in New Mexico—Frank's next assignment in the States.

I honestly hadn't thought about how Frank and I, considered a mixed-race couple, would be treated over there. The conversation just never came up. Mother never talked about it either. The only time Mother expressed an opinion about my going to America was when I asked for a copy of her birth certificate, which I needed for my visa. Mother was reluctant to contact the Registra in Ireland to get a copy of the certificate. When it arrived she thrust it in my hand saying, "Why can't ye marry an Englishman."

I never told my mother how much it meant for me to hold her birth certificate, written in both English and Irish, and to learn, for the first time, at age 20, the names of my grandparents—John and Sarah Halligan. I smiled when I saw my grandmother's name. Mother had given me her mother's name, Sarah, as my middle name. The discovery gave me a warm feeling. I had a small connection.

The week before I left for America, my family surprised me with a going-away tea. The bigger surprise occurred when Mother told me Doris had purchased and prepared the food, just as she did for my wedding reception. I don't think I thanked Doris this time either. My brother, Terry, who would later immigrate to Australia, gave me a present—a necklace with a cross pendant. I was shocked, and touched by his gift.

Mother (age 48), holding Tina (age 16 months), outside 84 Mannock Road before I left for the U.S. in 1965

My first passport (Age 20)

Entered New York April 1965

LOVING VS VIRGINIA

The huge British Airways jet, just like the one I'd seen during a John Lea School field trip, had just carried me and my two small children, a world away from England. Frank was unable to travel with us. His rank wasn't high enough to qualify for a military-paid family flight. The plane screeched to a halt on the tarmac of the John F. Kennedy International Airport in New York. The year was 1965 and I was 20-years-old, with two children under three. Had I travelled to New York two years earlier, I would have arrived at the Idlewide Airport. The Idlewild was renamed, John F. Kennedy, in memory of the 35th president who was assassinated two years earlier.

Resourceful, as always, Frank devised a plan to pay my way to the States. Airmen were allowed to purchase a substantial amount of inexpensive alcohol and cigarettes from the Base store. Frank would buy the maximum allowed, then sell it at a profit to some local people—a common practice among G.I.'s. The First Sergeant of Frank's unit had been alerted he'd exhausted his alcohol and cigarette rations every month—a red flag to those keeping track. Frank reported to me he looked his Sergeant in the eye, and told him he wasn't selling the stuff, he just had lots of house parties.

"I knew if I kept repeating this there was nothing they could do. How could they prove otherwise?" Frank said, pleased with himself.

I was afraid he'd get caught, but we both knew the money from these items was the only way the children and I would be able to travel from England to America, and join him at his next assignment at Kirtland Air force Base near Albuquerque, New Mexico. I was excited to be moving to a country which fascinated me ever since I could remember. The father I never knew was born there, and now I was going to live there.

When the children and I arrived in New York, my excitement was mingled with fatigue from trying to soothe the children during a nine-hour flight from London. After struggling through customs, I was relieved when an eager, muscular porter took charge of my luggage. He signaled for a taxicab, and then stood waiting. I knew nothing about tipping, and was unfamiliar with American money. Cradling my baby daughter in one arm, with my toddler son clinging to my leg, I rummaged through my purse, and gave the porter all the change I had. He looked at me with disgust. "You people travel around the world but you can't give a working guy a decent tip. I hope the cabby takes you for a ride."

I was confused, and frightened, and alone in New York City. Thank goodness the cab driver had better things to do than hold me, and two crying children, hostage. We were dropped off at our destination without an unsolicited tour of the city.

Juggling babies and bags, I transferred from the taxi to a large, black, U.S. Air Force limousine for the 1½-hour trip south to McGuire AFB in New Jersey, where Frank would join us the following day.

Several adults were already seated inside the limousine when we entered. The children were exhausted, pulling at their little ears which still hurt from the

"Fudge"

pressure during the plane's descent. I tried to comfort them, but they continued to whimper. One of the female passengers threw annoyed looks my way, and another asked me to keep the children quiet—as if I wasn't trying.

As the children drifted in and out of sleep, I stared out of the limousine window and my initial excitement began to return. Along the way the limousine pulled to a stop at an intersection where a policeman was directing traffic. This was the first time I'd seen an American policeman in the flesh, and although I knew police officers in the U.S. carried guns, I was stilled shocked to see a pistol up close. Our English Bobbies carried a whistle and a truncheon—a lot less frightening. The limousine glided to a stop at a hotel on the Base where the three of us would spend the night.

Frank decided we'd visit his mother in Roanoke, Virginia, before continuing on to the base in New Mexico. I had mixed feelings. The relationship between Frank and his mother had never been a warm one, and it became a lot cooler when he asked Alzona's permission to marry me.

I might have been able to persuade Frank to skip the Virginia visit, but I wanted Alzona to see her grandchildren, and hoped this would warm things up between Frank and his mother.

Alzona opened the door to her brick house and greeted each of us with a warm hug and a kiss. We entered her spacious, neat, living room and received another hug and kiss from Gene, Frank's older brother. Gene looked a lot like Frank, only heavier.

Alzona lifted both children on her lap calling them "doll babies," and kissed them, insisting they give her lots of "sugar" in return.

Frank's mother saw the confused look on my face when she referred to Frank by his middle name of "Ivan."

"I've always called him Ivan," she said, "I never wanted to be reminded of Frank, my louse of an ex-husband."

I could see where Frank got his outspokenness. Half the time, I had no idea who Alzona was talking to, or about. "Ivan" had been "Frank the Yank" to me for three years.

There was a strong physical resemblance between Frank and his mother. They had the same small, turned-up noses, and skin as white as the flesh of the backyard chicken after Mother plucked off the feathers. I guessed Alzona had once had the same light brown hair as Frank, and his brother. Now her hair was dyed, but not an unflattering red.

Frank was visiting old high school friends one evening leaving Alzona and me alone. Out of the blue she said, "I'm surprised you're as big as you are. Ivan always had tiny girlfriends."

My mouth dropped open. I didn't know how to respond. I was hardly the size of Tessie O'Shea (a very large singer Mother was fond of quoting). Even if I were heavy—who would say such a thing to someone's face? Alzona also had an earthy sense of humor. I've always been a bit prissy, and was horrified when she told me a dirty joke. I managed to squeak out a tight smile, and hoped it didn't look like a grimace.

How ironic, I thought. Here's this so-called genteel Southern woman, who'd delayed permission for her son to marry me—ostensibly because I wasn't good enough for him—and she's grossing me out. I couldn't wait to write and tell Mother.

Alzona followed up this startling conversation with a "Would you like some tea honey?"—in her lilting southern accent.

I was dying for a cuppa. Alzona returned from the kitchen with a tall glass filled with orange-colored liquid, and ice cubes. I didn't want to be rude, unlike some people, so I tried to gulp down as much of the stuff as I could. I had swallowed my first, and my last, glass of iced tea. I couldn't wait to write to my mother about this too.

After meeting Alzona, I was almost afraid to meet her three married sisters, who lived nearby. Once again, I was surprised and relieved, by the reception I got—they couldn't have been more refined, and generous. At each of their homes, we were showered with belated wedding gifts, and presents for the children. Frank's family, and friends, were fascinated by my British accent, and would listen in rapt silence whenever I opened my mouth. I was both flattered and bemused by this attention—I thought their soft southern accents much more attractive than my English accent.

Looking back, I'm sure my being a foreigner from England made it easier for them to accept me. I doubt I would have received as warm a welcome had I been a mixed-race American.

The American Civil Rights Act, outlawing segregation in schools and public places, had been signed by the time I arrived in 1965. What I didn't know, was something just as egregious, and incomprehensible, was still the law.

Racially-mixed marriages were not just socially unacceptable—they were illegal in at least 17 states—including the State of Virginia. When Alzona refused to give permission for Frank and me to marry, she was not just being bigoted—she was obeying the law. Not until two years later, in 1967, would these miscegenation laws be overturned. I'd read the couple responsible for challenging the system was two sweethearts—Mildred Jeter, who was a mix of Black and Native American, and Richard Loving, who was white.

Mildred was 18 when she became pregnant with Richard's baby. They were both born and raised in Virginia and knew they'd have to leave the state to marry. When they returned to Virginia, the police came to their home in the middle of the night and arrested them for "cohabiting as man and wife, against the peace and dignity of the Commonwealth."

They showed their marriage license, but Virginia's law banning interracial marriage, also applied if you married elsewhere, and returned to Virginia. The couple was found guilty as charged. The judge declared the "Almighty God" put the different races on separate continents so they wouldn't mix.

The couple lost several court appeals, and in a last ditch effort, Mildred wrote to Robert Kennedy, younger brother of the assassinated President, and Attorney General of the United States. The American Civil Liberties Union argued the case before the U.S. Supreme Court on April 10, 1967. The court, on June 12, 1967, declared Virginia's anti-miscegenation statute in violation of the "equal protection" fourteenth amendment, and thereby unconstitutional. This landmark decision served to end all race-based legal restrictions on marriage in the United States.

But this occurred in 1967, and I'd arrived in the U.S. in 1965. One evening, as Frank, Alzona, and I were cruising around their Virginia neighborhood, Frank pointed to a small brick house, and said he would like to buy it for us someday.

"You know you can't live here, Ivan," Alzona said.

Once again I was dumbfounded by her insensitivity. Frank was furious. When we arrived at his mother's house he flew in the door.

"We're leaving," he said.

I tried to calm him down, but nothing worked.

Frank wouldn't let me pack up any of the wedding presents, and even refused to take the children's gifts with us. Everyone, except Frank, cried as we left Alzona's house.

I had lots of time to think on the 1,600 mile train ride from Virginia to New Mexico. Frank was in denial, and responded with anger when faced with the fact we couldn't live in Virginia. I was also in denial, and wanted to keep the façade of acceptance. I knew we were never going to live in Virginia. To me it was the same as drinking the tall glass of awful ice tea—just smile and choke it down.

When we got off the train in Albuquerque I stood with the children by the station brick wall while Frank went to get a taxi. The heat emanating from the wall was hotter than the gas oven I used to stick my head in to dry my hair. I couldn't wait to write and tell Mother. I embraced the dry desert heat. What a difference from the cold, wet English climate. Besides enjoying the warmth, I could style my hair and it would stay styled—no horrible humidity to destroy my efforts. A small thing in the scheme of things, but it meant a lot to me.

We moved into a one-story apartment complex filled with air force families. The flat-roofed buildings were painted a light grey, with bleached pebbles and an occasional cactus for landscaping. After dinner the adults would sit outside on the communal picnic benches smoking cigarettes and sipping cold beverages. Our young children chased darting fireflies as the sun went down and the air cooled.

I took advantage of the air force's dependent education program and attended the AAA Business College in town. I struggled learning how to touch type. Despite my early success playing two-ball as a child, hand-eye coordination tasks were never easy for me. I made friends with a few of the young women students, most of whom were just out of high school. As we sat together eating lunch in an outdoor café, their talk was all about who they were dating. Their heads would swivel when a noisy GTO muscle car zoomed by. They'd jump up and wave to the handsome teen-age driver with his window down, and his cigarette packet rolled up in the sleeve of his white T-shirt. What a carefree life they had. I was only twenty but felt so much older.

I eventually passed the typing and shorthand tests, and was prepared to go to work. Those plans were delayed when Frank got orders to go to Vietnam. I was sorry he was going into a war zone, but not as sorry as I should have been. We were still arguing a lot, and neither of us was happy in the marriage. I can't put my finger on why our marriage was so contentious. We didn't argue about big things like money, or infidelity, or addiction. There just seemed to be a constant low level of dissatisfaction. Something was missing for both of us.

After spending a little over a year in New Mexico, Frank shipped out to Vietnam, and I was on my way back to England. It was 1966.

Alzona with
Dean
(2yrs.4months)

Roanoke,
Virginia
1965

THE OLIVE TWIG

I met Willie G., Doris' husband, when I returned to England while Frank was in Vietnam. Willie was from Little Rock, Arkansas, a place which carries an indelible stain of racial prejudice.

I'd been distressed and confused as a 13 year-old, watching those frightening scenes on our black and white telly in Wellingborough. Crowds of angry white people filled the screen waving Southern flags. They carried signs reading: "We won't go to school with Negroes." They screamed racial slurs—their faces contorted with rage.

I couldn't understand the depth of the hatred I was seeing and hearing. I'd been subjected to name-calling from ignorant kids, but these people were adults. Even the Arkansas Governor, Orval Faubus, supported this hatred. He'd called out the state's National Guard to prevent nine African-American students from attending Little Rock High School, even though racial segregation in schools had been banned in 1954 under the Supreme Court ruling, "Brown v Board of Education." President Eisenhower was forced to send in Federal troops from the 101st Airborne Division to ensure the safety of the young students, and to escort them to their state's high school.

My brother, Terry, who was also watching the program back then, blurted out, "Pauline shouldn't be going to school with us then."

It would've been just like me to kick Terry in the shins, and bolt out the back door. Ironically, after I married and was leaving for the U.S. for the first time, Terry was the only one who gave me a goodbye present.

Although the state of Arkansas conjured up ugly images from the past, I didn't hold this against Doris' husband, Willie. After all, my husband was also white, and from the South.

The icy relationship between Doris and me had thawed due to our living thousands of miles apart—me in New Mexico, and she in England. Also, knowing how Doris thought, I was now respectable—married with two children, and what's more, I had a husband serving his country in Vietnam.

Doris and Willie lived in a bungalow on the other side of Wellingborough from Mother's house, where I was staying. Doris invited the children and me to her house for tea one afternoon. For reasons I couldn't fathom, Doris' approval mattered to me. The few times in the past when she'd offered an olive twig, I'd accepted, and I did again.

The children and I stepped off the bus, and were making our way to Doris' house, when we saw her walking toward us. As she drew closer, I could see she had a serious look on her face. I felt anxious. Doris normally greeted my children with a big smile.

"Willie's sergeant from the Base dropped in," she said.

I stood there, puzzled. Doris made no attempt to walk us back to her house. Then the penny dropped. She didn't want me to come to the house because Willie's boss was there. They were ashamed of me—the half-black sister.

I turned around and hurried back to the bus stop, fighting to control the tears so the children wouldn't be upset. Doris had inflicted years of emotional pain on me,

"Fudge"

but this insult hurt the most. I had opened myself up.

When I walked into Mother's house, the tears I hoped to control spurted from my eyes.

"What happened?" my mother asked anxiously. I told her.

"Who the f--k do these Yanks think they are?" she said, placing the blame on Willie, and forgetting for the moment that Doris had always been ashamed I was her sister.

Several weeks later during a conversation with my little sister, Delly, she told me that after I left England for the first time, she became the target of Doris' abusive remarks. It was then that I understood. The bile had always been inside Doris, and had nothing to do with me. I was just a convenient target.

Doris' wedding day. Wellingborough, 1966
The closest we ever came to a family photograph

Back row(L-R): Kevan and fiancée Heather, Eileen, Sheila and husband Pete
Center(L-R): Unknown best man, Willie, Doris, Sid, Terry, and Mother
Front row(L-R): Donna (Sheila's daughter), and Delly
Missing: Malcolm, Sheila's son Richard, Billy, and me.

ONE ENCHANTED EVENING

My year back in England went quickly while Frank was in Vietnam. I rented a house in Earls Barton, a small town a ten-minute bus ride from Mother. I dutifully wrote to Frank, and he was responsible about sending money. More than once I thought about divorcing him and staying in England, but I couldn't bring myself to do it while he was in Vietnam. I'd read about wives and girlfriends ditching their men while they were over there, and I couldn't be one of them.

Toward the end of his Vietnam tour, Frank wrote he'd received orders for Randolph Air Force Base near San Antonio, Texas. I had a formal photograph taken of me and the kids for Mother, and then I was back on a plane and off on another adventure. Frank and I reunited in Texas, but in the one year absence our hearts hadn't grown fonder. We quickly reverted to our pattern of bickering.

Despite our rocky marriage we still tried to make a go

of it, and even purchased a small house near the Base. I felt comfortable living in Texas with its large, brown-skinned Hispanic population.

My neighbor two doors down was from London, and Beryl and I became good friends. She would call me each morning and say, "Ready for some coffee mate," and we'd both laugh at the play on words. One morning I answered Beryl's usual phone call and she was laughing.

"You'll never guess what I heard," she said. "You know the neighbors who just moved in between us? Well she came over to say hello last night and she said 'Guess who's living next door to us—a goddam Mexican.'"

It took me a minute to realize the neighbor was talking about me. I joined in Beryl's laughter. Both of us could only image what this neighbor would have said had she known my true racial identify.

After a year in Texas, Frank received his requested re-assignment to England. The children and I stayed with my mother while Frank looked for a place to live near his assigned base near Felixstowe, on England's East Coast, about a hundred miles from Wellingborough.

It didn't take long for me to realize Frank wasn't in any hurry for me and the children to join him. He said he had difficulty finding a suitable rental. I was anxious to have a place of my own, so I told him when I was coming to Felixstowe. Miraculously, he found a house within a month.

It was a mistake. We lasted less than six months. A series of events occurred where I had to protect the children. British police have no jurisdiction over American Servicemen, so I telephoned Frank's superior officer. Frank was ordered out of our house and into the Bentwaters Air Force Base barracks. Our six-year tumultuous relationship was finally over.

"Fudge"

Our separation would not have come as a surprise to anyone who knew us when we were dating. The red flags had been waving from the beginning. Both of us had less than ideal upbringings. Frank's mother, Alzona, had been married three times, and the stepfathers had been physically cruel to Frank, and his older brother Gene. I'd been raised by a violent, hard-drinking Irishman, and suffered years of emotional abuse from my sister, Doris. Both of us were scarred.

After Frank was forced to move into the barracks, I couldn't afford the rental house and moved into a cheaper place. My apartment was the upstairs of a terraced house overlooking the North Sea. The lower apartment was rented by a young American couple, Don and Anne, who had a lovely little baby girl, who, ironically had been born with one arm—just like my sister, Sheila.

I quickly found work through a temporary hiring agency that placed me in various office jobs at the Felixstowe docks. I didn't have a telephone so my work assignments would arrive by telegram. My New Mexico business college training was finally paying off. I was the happiest I'd been in years. I had two great kids, regular employment, and a group of supportive American friends.

If you knew who Mama Cass Elliot was, then you'd have a picture of Georgia, an American woman who became one of my closest friends. Georgia had flowing straight black hair, a gregarious personality, and a large frame covered with an ever-present poncho. She managed to squeeze herself into a yellow Volkswagen Bug, which she drove at breakneck speed around the narrow village streets between her apartment and Bentwaters Air force Base, where her husband Jeff was stationed. Their two children, Trina and Buddie, became friends with my two children.

Georgia's flat was just a few streets away from mine. Her door was always open and friends moved freely in and out. Something was always bubbling on the stove. I was made welcome, and felt safe—just what the kids and I needed.

I'd told a white lie to the landlord, Mr. Unthank, so he'd rent the apartment to me. Georgia had warned me he only rented to married couples. I told Mr. Unthank I was married—which was true—but let him believe I was living with my husband—which wasn't true. Mr. Unthank became suspicious when, no matter when he came to collect the rent, there was no man around.

"Where's your husband?" he would inquire, peering around me as he stood on the front doorstep, "He never seems to be home."

"He's on temporary duty in Italy," I'd lie.

This worked for a time. Someone, probably Frank, told Mr. Unthank I was separated from my husband.

"You'll have to move out," he informed me one day. "I don't rent to single people."

I was devastated. I'd made a nice home for me and the children. The flat was in walking distance to my jobs at the Felixstowe docks. Anne, the young wife who lived in the downstairs flat, would watch the children for the short time they'd be home from school before I got off work. I couldn't have asked for a more perfect arrangement.

I ran all the way to Georgia's house to break the news.

"We'll see about that," Georgia said.

She gathered together all the wives who she knew were renting from this same landlord.

"We're going to tell Unthank that if he evicts Pauline, we'll all move out—all four families."

The women slowly nodded their head in agreement—

except for one—Ellen, Georgia's downstairs neighbor.

"I don't think I can go along with this," Ellen said, "Glen's overseas and I don't think he'd like it."

Georgia threw her a look of disgust.

"For God's sake Ellen—nothing is going to happen. The old fool will back down if we all stick together."

Ellen nodded weakly and off we all went—a striking contingent of loyal friends. We trailed after Georgia as she marched down her apartment steps, and out the door towards her yellow bug, poncho flapping. Several of us squeezed in beside and behind her, and off we sped.

Mr. Unthank lived in a massive brick house, large enough to accommodate all our families. He answered the door bell. A look of astonishment crossed his face when he saw the motley crew of young women squeezed onto his doorstep.

Georgia stated our case. "Pauline is a good tenant. She's quiet and she pays her rent on time, every month. She even painted the kitchen and living room using her own money to buy paint."

I cringed when Georgia mentioned the painting—I wasn't sure it was allowed.

"If she's out, we're all out," Georgia said, sounding a lot like Paddy Fleming the shop steward in my favorite television sitcom, "The Rag Trade," whose catchphrase was, "Everybody Out."

Mr. Unthank didn't say a word. We waited quietly as he looked each woman in the eye, avoiding my stare. Georgia had Ellen's arm in a vice grip to help her stand firm. As Georgia predicted, Unthank relented. "Okay, she can stay. But if there are any problems I'm coming to see you, Georgia."

Georgia ignored the remark and we turned and fled before he changed his mind.

The incident reminded me of another occasion when someone stood up for me. I operated a machine called a skiver, in one of my first shoe factory jobs. My task involved shaving off enough leather from the upper part of a shoe section so the sewing machine operator could stich it to the lower section. If I didn't take enough leather off the upper, it would be too thick for the machinists' needle. If I took too much off, holes would appear and I had to toss the leather in a waste bucket. I was inept, and consistently skived off too much leather creating more waste than anyone in the factory. I became a liability. The factory foreman, the only male in the building, fired me. I was holding my last pay packet, and crying, when our neighbor, Mrs. Shaw, approached me and discovered I'd been sacked. She marched straight over to the foreman.

"You can't give Pauline the sack. If you do, we're all out."

The foreman relented, and re-hired me. I don't know if Mr. Unthank in Felixstowe, or the shoe factory foreman in Wellingborough, actually took these threats of walk-outs seriously. Perhaps they just admired and respected the loyalty of these women. I know I did.

When Georgia wasn't throwing a house party, she was going to one. She convinced me to go with her to a going-away party for someone I didn't know.

Rock music blared—courtesy of the pirate ship, Radio Caroline, moored off the British coast where it was safely out of clutches of the monopolizing British Broadcasting Corporation. Georgia disappeared almost as soon as we arrived at the party. I circulated among people I didn't know, and eventually squeezed myself on the edge of a

"Fudge"

settee occupied by three other people. I felt uncomfortable, but fixed a face I hoped looked like I was enjoying myself. I wasn't looking to meet anyone that night. In fact, I'd been trying to get rid of someone for weeks.

A month earlier I'd applied for a legal separation from Frank—a required step in England at the time, before an eventual divorce could be granted. Frank and I were living apart and arrived at the hearing separately. Frank drove up in his large, grey American Oldsmobile—disparagingly called "the yank tank" by the villagers who had to press themselves against the side of shop buildings when he drove by, occupying both lanes of the narrow road. I walked to the hearing.

A man and a woman sat on one side of a long, shiny, wooden table, and Frank and I sat apart from each other on the other side—facing the hearing officers who were shuffling papers. We each gave a statement as to why we should be granted the legal separation—the details I have long forgotten, but not the officials' response. They advised Frank and me to go out and have a nice dinner. Our request for a legal separation had been refused.

Frank smirked as we left the room, as if he had somehow won—then he drove off as I walked home totally bewildered. I decided the hearing officers were nuts, mentally declared myself divorced, and proceeded to act accordingly.

So here I was, at this house party, trading sideways glances with a young man sitting across the crowded room. He wasn't Rossano Brazzi, and I wasn't exactly Mitzi Gaynor—the two stars of *South Pacific*—but I did "see a stranger across a crowded room." The stranger and I limited our communication to quick looks, and I left the party without even knowing his name, although I did overhear someone call him "JJ." The next time I saw Georgia, I confided to her I'd found this "JJ" attractive, and learned from her he'd inquired about me.

Georgia turned up at my apartment the following weekend and whisked me off to the base to meet "JJ." I learned his name was Jim. He'd told Georgia's husband he wanted to talk to me, but mistakenly thought the man I was squeezed next to on the sofa was my date. We began our short courtship. Short, because Jim had only a few months left in England before his overseas assignment and his four-year military service commitment would end, and he'd return to California. This looming departure date may have had a lot to do with how quickly we became attached to each other. Jim didn't seem concerned about my marital status; knowing he was on his way out of the country may have helped.

I liked that Jim didn't want to just spend time with me—he often included the children. We'd walk hand-in-hand on the Felixstowe beach, the kids running on ahead taking turns chasing each other, laughing as they fought against the bitter breeze from the North Sea. I knew then that I didn't need a lot to feel happy. Being with a calm, kind person was enough. One day, as the four of us strolled around the neighborhood together, Jim picked a pink rambling rose that hung over a fence. He handed it to Tina and said, "When I see a rose, I'll think of you." They say the way to a man's heart is through his stomach. The way to my heart was through my children.

Jim promised to write—a pledge Karen, one of my more cynical friends, warned me to take with a grain of salt.

I was content with my life in the small seaside town. My kids were healthy, happy, and doing very well in school. I had an enjoyable social life—but I missed Jim. I

"Fudge"

wasn't interested in dating anyone else.

A week after Jim left, I let out a shout of joy when I picked up the postcard the postman had slid through the mail slot in the front door. The card depicted the iconic Statue of Liberty in New York Harbor. Jim had mailed it when he'd arrived in New York. He'd kept his promise to write. A letter followed several weeks later. Jim invited me and the children to California.

FRIENDS AND FAMILY

One Saturday afternoon, shortly after hearing from Jim, the children and I took our weekly walk on the rocky North Sea beach and up the hill to Georgia's apartment. Georgia opened the door with her usual exuberant, "Hi guys." We entered her kitchen filled with the savory smell of something simmering. Dean and Tina scooted off to the back bedroom to play with Trini and Buddie. Georgia and I sat at the kitchen table.

"Are you still serious about going to California?" she asked, as she pulled a long strand of black hair out of her eyes.

"Yes, I am," I said.

Georgia handed me a thick envelope. I opened it and pulled out a wad of American money. Before I could speak, Georgia told me our group of friends had pitched in to help pay for my trip to the U.S. I cried.

I was still legally married to Frank, despite my efforts to get a divorce. This meant the air force would not have paid for me to return to the United States without my husband.

I managed to keep my pending move a secret from Frank. He'd proven he could be vindictive, and would've tried to stop me. My co-workers at the Felixstowe docks gave me a going-away party. They wished me well, but expressed concerns. Their worries had nothing to do with racial issues.

"America is such a violent country," someone had said. "They assassinated their president. Just two years ago they assassinated Martin Luther King and Bobby Kennedy."

Several co-workers thought California was the Wild West. "Americans are shooting each other all the time," said one friend.

"Isn't California sliding into the Pacific, and aren't you worried about the earthquakes?" said another. I wasn't worried.

My Mother came to stay with me for a couple of days before I left for the U.S., and added to the cacophony of doom.

"You're mad," she said, never one to mince words, "dragging the kids back there when you've only just met the man."

I felt I could trust Jim. He'd been kind and thoughtful to me and the children. I'd also learned something about Jim which bolstered my opinion of him.

On one of our dates, Jim arranged for me and the children to stay with him for a weekend, in a friend's caravan in Great Yarmouth, a town just up the coast, and more of a seaside resort than Felixstowe. Great Yarmouth actually had sand on its beach. When we arrived, Jim and the kids got out of the car to get the caravan keys from the resort manager. Jim slammed the car door shut and the vibration jolted open the glove compartment in front where I sat. A blue airmail envelope caught my eye. I reached for it, and pulled the letter from the opened envelope. I scanned the neatly written words while anxiously keeping an eye out for Jim and the kids.

The letter began, "My dearest Jim," and went on to talk about family activities, and signed, "All our love, Mom and Dad." *He had a loving family.* This might seem like flimsy proof of a person's character to some, but it bolstered my opinion of Jim as a nice guy, and one who could be trusted.

The kids and I flew off to America in December 1970, a couple of weeks before Christmas.

The money donated by my American friends in England, coupled with my own meagre savings, was enough to fly us to New York, but not to California. The kids and I took the less expensive Greyhound Bus the rest of the way. Although I'd lived in the States before, I didn't comprehend the size of the country.

It took three days to journey from New York, on the East Coast, to Sacramento, California, on the West Coast. The children and I slept on the bus, and at times in the bus terminals—which were well-kept in the small towns, but often dirty and scary in the big cities where we'd step over vagrants sleeping on the floor. I wasn't used to seeing people lying around like that. Unlike in England, where everybody rode the bus, public transportation in America, and in particular Greyhound, is mostly used by the poor.

Jim met us at the Greyhound bus station on L Street in downtown Sacramento. The shiny fire-engine red Chevelle Super Sport car looked even more striking than it appeared in the photograph Jim had proudly shown me in England. He'd purchased the car in 1966, just before being shipped to England on a four-year tour, and apparently his parents had taken very good care of it. As we drove out of the town center I turned around to check on Dean and Tina in the back seat. They were giggling and talking about the car—the booming dual exhausts on this 396 fiery four-speed had brought smiles to the faces of my weary young children. They'd been angels on the trip—no bickering or complaining, even though the three

"Fudge"

of us had traveled almost 3,000 miles together.

After a few carefree weeks together in the apartment Jim had rented, he and I were forced to face the reality of our financial situation. I only had a few dollars, and Jim didn't have much more. He was competing for jobs with thousands of returning veterans who, like him, had completed their four-year military draft. Jim could have returned to his job at The Campbell Soup Company where he worked before being drafted, but he'd risen to the rank of staff sergeant in less than three years in the air force, and a mundane factory job had little appeal to him. He also told me he wasn't about to wear a hairnet over his lengthening hippie locks—a requirement in the soup factory.

Our two-story apartment complex was located in the south side of Sacramento, not far from Burbank High where Jim went to school. The complex was nicknamed Sin City by the locals. Jim said it earned its reputation because it was one of the few places in the area that rented to unmarried couples.

With Christmas just a week away, I was anxious to bring some holiday cheer to the apartment. The decorations came from some unlikely places.

Jim had grown up camping in the Sierra Nevada—a mountain range that spans 400 miles from north to south along the eastern edge of California. He was excited to show me and the children Hope Valley—one of the lush high-mountain meadows where his family pitched their tents and fished for Rainbow Trout in the sparkling snow-melt streams.

The powerful red Chevy easily climbed the winding Highway 50. "This brings back memories," Jim said as he deftly shifted into third gear. "My dad had a Volkswagen

Bug. The car was packed to the headliner with our camping gear. Mom was in the front, and my two brothers and I were in the back. This was in the fifties before this highway was built, and we had to take two-lane roads from downtown Sacramento to the mountains. Since my brother, Ray, and I were the two oldest kids, anytime we reached a hill, my dad would tell us to jump out of the car to lighten the load. We'd chase each other up the hill ahead of the Bug, which was sputtering behind us. Our baby brother, Mike, lounging in the back seat, would be grinning like a Cheshire cat." We all laughed.

On our return trip down the mountain road, Jim pulled over into a turnout on the highway. As the children and I stretched our legs and gazed out at the snow-capped mountains and forests of pine trees, Jim wandered off a short distance away. He returned carrying a small fir tree. The kids laughed and clapped their hands. We had our Christmas tree.

With the tree stashed safely in the trunk, the four of us clambered back in the car. Jim burned rubber as we swiftly left the area to avoid being arrested by a forest ranger.

Back in the apartment, Jim nailed the miniature tree to the small wooden cross he'd made for support, and proudly displayed it on the vinyl kitchen tabletop. The small apartment was soon filled with the popping sound, and the toasty smell, of roasted corn kernels. Jim had made popcorn in the cast-iron skillet given to us by his mother. He demonstrated how to string the puffy kernels together with a needle and thread, and wound it around the tree—a holiday decoration new to me and the kids. Jim spent the rest of the evening trying to pop enough corn to replace what the kids kept eating.

The four of us stood back from the table to admire the

"Fudge"

decorated tree. Jim said it needed something. He tore the flap off a cardboard box and cut it into the shape of a star. He showed the kids how to cover it with aluminum foil, and then tied it to the top of the tree. If there were any gift exchanges between us, they have long been forgotten.

We accepted Jim's parents' invitation to Christmas dinner. I hadn't been in any hurry to meet them. Although California was a long way from Virginia, geographically and culturally, I was apprehensive. I could imagine what Jim's parents thought about me. I wasn't exactly what a parent would choose for their adored eldest son—I was a foreigner of questionable racial heritage, married to another man, three years older than their son, had two school-age children, and was willing to live in Sin City.

If Jim's parents had any negative thoughts or feelings toward me, they managed to hide them. Roger opened the front door wide, and he and Betty greeted us with smiles—they were not huggers back then. We shared a bountiful Christmas dinner with them, and Jim's fifteen-year-old brother, Mike. After we ate, Roger and Betty disappeared into the garage and returned wheeling two shiny new bikes. Dean and Tina literally jumped for joy.

I'd discover in the following weeks Jim's mother was a lot friendlier than her impassive face, and pulled-back French roll hairdo portrayed. She laughed easily and seemed to enjoy my children's company. Betty willingly shared her favorite recipes with me, and often invited us to dinner knowing how broke we were. Some time later, when Betty and I began sharing our life experiences, I'd learn she was the daughter of French Basque immigrants, and spoke only French when she first went to school. She was ridiculed by some of the other students because of this. She told me the kids called her a french fry. Compared to the names I was called as a child, a french fry didn't sound too terrible, but it underscored how any hurtful name which serves to mark a child as different, can be devastating.

Betty's only sister, Grace, and her husband, Jack, and their two children, Don and Linda, were warm and friendly the minute we met, and Grace has playfully teased me ever since. Jim's Basque grandfather, "Poppa," loved to tease the children, and me. Tina would lie on the floor and put her bare foot on Poppa's lap. He'd twist her big toe. She'd squeal, pull her foot away and seconds later put it back on his lap.

"How old is she anyway, Yimmy?" Poppa said one day to Jim, loud enough for me to hear. His French accent was still strong after five decades in America, and he couldn't pronounce his "J's."

I thought he was criticizing our relationship because I was three years older than Jim, and had children. My feelings were hurt. Then Poppa turned around and I could see the twinkle in his blue eyes.

"He only teases the people he likes," Jim told me later.

I'd wish I'd been able to meet Poppa's beautiful Basque wife, Marie, but she died in her thirties of leukemia when Jim's mother was only 16. We have their wedding photograph hanging in our hallway.

Betty had three handsome, dark-haired brothers: Bob, Dick, and Bernie. Uncle Dick was divorced and struggling to support the five children in his custody: Rick, Vicky, Kathy, Brad and Michelle. He generously shared with us some of the surplus government food he'd received. Dick, and Jim's parents, gave us their surplus furniture when we upgraded from Sin City to an unfurnished place. Jim's childhood friend, Susie Pope, and her husband Bud, chipped in with a small television. These items, along with Jim's prized stereo equipment, were everything we needed.

I was in awe as to how many cousins Jim had, and they all lived close by. Eight cousins, which included Shawna—Uncle Bernie's daughter—all lived in Stockton. There were more cousins in other nearby towns: Carol and Cindy, who lived in Lodi, and four cousins in Loomis: Jerry, Sharon, Tom, and Anita. I counted 14 cousins, and at least 9 aunts and uncles. This total didn't include those relatives in the State of Oregon, and who knows where else. I compared this abundance of loving relatives with my scant three uncles and three cousins. Without exception, Jim's family and friends embraced me and my children.

STICKS AND STONES

Within weeks of arriving in Sacramento we'd enrolled Dean and Tina in school. Both children excelled in every subject—the result of an excellent early education at St. Peter's, a private school in Felixstowe. They soon made friends, and were accepted by the American children, with the occasional exception. One day, after several weeks in the new school, Tina came home in tears. "Mummy," she sobbed, "the kids keep calling me an English muffin."

I hugged her, and was able to suppress a smile as I thought about the names I'd been called as a child. But just like Jim's mother's "french fry" taunt—Tina had been singled out as different, and it hurt her. When she was in her teens something more troubling happened. Tina was not only a very pretty child, she was also very smart—a combination which apparently upset some of the girls in her Junior High School.

"A gang of Mexican girls pushed me around today," she told me nonchalantly as we were doing the dishes after dinner one evening. "They called me a white bitch."

I gasped. Before I could catch my breath, Tina went on. "Last week a couple of white girls yelled at me and called out, 'Hey you dirty Mexican.'"

I stared at Tina in disbelief. She didn't look the least bit upset by this verbal abuse.

"Fudge"

"How long has this stuff been going on?" I asked, ready to tear off to hunt down the culprits."

"Don't worry mum," she'd said with a slight smile. "I secretly liked that they thought I was different ethnicities. I felt kind of exotic."

Because of her fair skin, straight brown hair, and hazel eyes—Tina's African heritage was imperceptible, protecting her from the nasty racial slurs I'd experienced. My son, Dean, who had similar skin coloring to his sister, was less likely to share his feelings, so I never knew if he, too, suffered racial taunts. I never asked.

Less than a month after I arrived in Sacramento, I was working as a receptionist and bookkeeper for J.V. Equipment Company, a business that sold large meat tenderizing equipment. I liked my job, and would have stayed there longer had Jim not encouraged me apply for a government job. Sacramento is the capital of California—a fact I didn't know until I met Jim—and the city's largest employer.

I thought I was ineligible to work for State Government since I wasn't an American citizen. I'd learn that as a "registered alien,"—a term that never failed to amuse my children—I could work for the State, just not the Federal Government.

With more than 300 State Government agencies, it was sheer good luck, that after I successfully passed a state exam, a random selection landed me an interview with the California State Department of Water Resources. The Department was managed by registered engineers, and had a reputation for being both professional and highly organized—qualities not commonly attributed to government entities.

My interview for a Clerk/Typist position was on the

11th floor of the 13-story Resources Building, in the heart of downtown Sacramento—just streets away from the domed State Capitol building. After an interview with Erlene Clark, the slim, animated, young clerical supervisor, she pushed back her chair, and motioned me to follow her down a corridor to a room with a sign that read: Executive Typing Pool. The door opened to a room full of young women, seated in rows, their fingers rapidly tapping the keys of typewriters parked on grey metal desks. Erlene's desk faced the typists, giving the area the appearance of a school room.

The clickety clacking ceased when Erlene faced the typists, and raised her hand. She introduced me to the group, and then led me down an aisle to chat with a few of the staff. After the pool door closed behind us, Erlene turned to me and said, "I think you'll fit in." Apparently I'd been hired.

It was 1972, and personal office computers were a decade away from common business use. I learned that every letter that left the typing pool for the signature of Director William Gianelli, or his deputies, had to be perfect. The use of Wite-Out correction fluid, or correction tape was not allowed. I'd mastered touch typing at the New Mexico business college, but wasn't what you'd call an expert typist. To confirm this, at the end of the work day, the waste basket beside my desk was filled with discarded papers. I was so embarrassed I sneaked half the trash home with me. At times I'd have flashbacks to my leather skiving days in the Wellingborough shoe factory where I demonstrated a similar ineptitude. Fortunately, Erlene was patient, unlike my factory supervisor, and in time my typing accuracy improved.

To ensure that letters reflected the executives' drafts, they were required to be proofread by two people. The person who typed the letter read out loud from the original draft, while another checked the typed page. When I was the one who read, I was often faced with puzzled looks, followed by giggles, when I finished reading a sentence and ended with, "full stop."

"What's a 'full stop?'" I was asked—quickly followed with, "Oh, you mean 'a period.'"

My "inverted commas," were corrected to "quotation marks,"—"brackets" to "parentheses," and so it went on. My British accent was cause for teasing too, but it was light-hearted and complimentary—unlike my experience with my first husband. In time I caught on. It was like learning another language.

Across the corridor from the typing pool were the offices of the director, three deputies, and their personal secretaries. Typists from the pool were required to sit at the desks of the executive secretaries when they took their morning and afternoon breaks—their desks could never be left unattended. On occasion I was asked by one of the deputies to take dictation. I'd been promoted to Stenographer, but had little opportunity to practice shorthand since leaving college seven years earlier. I was relieved the letters were short.

By this time I'd worked for Water Resources for three years, and the new director was Ronald B. Robie, appointed by Democratic Governor, Jerry Brown. It was customary, following political party changes, that heads of State agencies—who were all political appointees—would also change. Former Director Gianelli had been appointed by Ronald Reagan, a Republican Governor. Six years later, in 1981, Reagan would become the Nation's 40th President. I saw Reagan once, when he was Governor. He'd entered the Resources Building with an entourage. He was as handsome as his photographs, but I was struck by his coloring. His skin looked a brownish orange—as if he'd just stepped off a stage.

Director Robie shook things up right away. He declared, "An open door policy,"—allowing employees at any level to schedule a meeting with him. This was modified, after a time, when his appointment calendar filled up with a bunch of whiners with an axe to grind about their supervisors. Edicts that stuck were Mr. Robie's insistence that managers answer their own telephones, and cease having their secretaries screen calls. He insisted that staff call him "Ron," and that everyone be on a first-name basis. I almost choked when I was asked to stop calling Assistant Director Charles Shoemaker, "Mr. Shoemaker," and refer to him instead as "Chuck." I would have found "Charles" more palatable.

There were other more profound changes in the Department, and throughout State Government. Affirmative Action, prescribed as an antidote to past discrimination and designed to increase the hiring of women and minorities, was in full swing. I may have been a beneficiary. This was something that didn't occur to me until I was introduced to a visitor, by one of the Executive Secretaries. Smiling proudly, she introduced me as, "Chuck's black secretary." I had my usual response to racial comments—stunned silence.

Although I had designated myself as "black" on various employment forms—and became a member of the department's Black Advisory Board—I felt a like an imposter. I looked the part, but I wasn't even an American, let alone an African-American. Nothing I endured in England compared to the systemic racial violence, oppression and bigotry suffered by black people in America.

The first time I designated a racial category I felt very

uncomfortable, it seemed so strange. I'd had a visceral reaction when I saw my first American birth certificate with a space for "race." This seemed akin to classifying an animal for entry into the Westminster Kennel Club Dog Show.

Director Robie's progressive changes echoed the winds blowing throughout the State of California in the 1970s. Governor Brown made a number of environmental activist appointments, including Claire Dedrick as Secretary of the State Resources Agency. Secretary Dedrick was the administrative head over all the natural resource commissions, boards, and departments—including Water Resources. All of us jumped when the "Agency" called.

One morning, I was asked by Erlene to hand a note directly to Mr. Robie who was meeting with the Secretary, in her office located two floors up. I was a respectful employee, but I almost lost my composure after entering Secretary Dedrick's inner office. A wicker chair, that resembled a cradle, was dangling from the ceiling. Gone was the standard, highly-polished. executive desk and straight back chairs. The Director and the Secretary were conducting their meeting seated on a comfy cushion-strewn couch.

Not surprisingly, Governor Brown, and many of his political appointees, received mixed reactions from the public, and the media. His Department of Transportation Director, Adrianna Gianturco, was referred to derisively as "the giant turkey," because of her highway decisions that included stopping the completion of a freeway interchange (literally in midair), and by restricting the fast lane of the busy Santa Monica freeway to cars with multiple occupants. The latter decision was reportedly decided by a previous administration, but left to Adrianna to enact, and subsequently get the blame.

The environmentalists' loved the Governor. Mike Royko, a syndicated *Chicago Sun-Times* columnist, did not. He enshrined Brown's nickname of "Governor Moonbeam." California was seen by many outside the State, and some inside, as a collection of eccentrics. Royko referred to the Golden State as, "the world's largest outdoor mental asylum." I, for one, was proud to be one of its inmates.

Although I had that one opportunity to enter Secretary Dedrick's office, I'd never stepped inside Director Robie's office until late one afternoon when I was instructed by Erlene to go to the Director's office to take dictation—his secretary had left early that day.

Mr. Robie was not a tall man, but he was well-proportioned. I'd often seen him hurrying passed the typing pool window with his head down, glasses perched on his nose, and an intense look on his face. That look would change quickly to a boyish grin whenever he greeted anyone.

Director Robie stood up from his desk chair as I entered his office clutching my spiral-bound stenographer's notebook. He gave me a cheery greeting—using my first name—and beckoned me to sit at a small, round cherrywood table just inside the door. Mr. Robie was an animated speaker. He spoke quickly, and paced. A few minutes into the dictation I heard a faint knocking. The Director showed no sign he'd heard anything. I realized I was making the noise. I was so nervous my knees were knocking the underside of the table. When Mr. Robie took an infrequent breath, I'd quickly go back over my notes and transcribe some of the words into longhand for fear I wouldn't be able to read them later. It was a long

"Fudge"

letter. I became more and more nervous. I imagined myself stuck in the typing pool for hours, struggling to transcribe my dictation while the Director paced outside. After he finished dictating, and to my everlasting gratitude, the Director looked at me and said, "It's Friday. I don't need this until Monday." I might have skipped out of his office. I took the steno pad home and spent most of the weekend deciphering my shorthand.

I could not have imagined, that 23 years later, in 1998, then Superior Court Judge, Ronald B. Robie, would graciously agree to conduct a private swearing-in ceremony for my daughter, Tina, and her friend, Alicia—admitting them to the California State Bar and a license to practice law.

I was proud that all three of my children graduated from college, particularly since my higher education dreams were dashed at age 11. My college aspirations were rekindled when a friend, Jo Silva, who was just a few years younger than I was, began attending the local college. I was inspired. Ten years of part-time college and I received my degree. I carried my graduation photograph with me on one of my trips home, and left it on top of my mother's bedroom dresser the morning I left to return to the States. Although I did well in school as a child, my mother never praised me. The highest compliment I received was overhearing her conversation over the hedge with Mrs. Cook when she whispered, "Pauline is doing ever so well in school."

All things seemed possible in California. A person could start college at any age. There was no test to determine your academic fate before the age of 12. A person's accent didn't categorize one as "working class," nor hinder their aspirations to move up the social and economic ladder. There were certainly other discriminatory barriers in California at this time, covert racism, ageism, and sexual orientation bias, to name a few, but the state was in the forefront of passing laws to prevent these practices. I'm certain my English accent protected me from racial discrimination—it tended to confuse people—and it was an asset in my early career as a secretary, judging from the compliments I received.

My Department of Water Resources' annual employee appraisals confirmed that my work habits were more than adequate, and it wasn't just my accent that advanced me to the managerial level. I found coordinating the work of others to be a task I enjoyed—with the occasional exceptions.

One of the secretaries, in a unit I supervised, went on a one-year maternity leave. I hired a young black woman as a temporary replacement. Shortly after she was hired I was asked to meet with the manager of the Equal Employment Office. The young woman had filed a discrimination complaint. My mouth dropped open when I read the charges. She claimed that my boss—a smart articulate man who could qualify for Mr. Congeniality—had directed a racial slur at her. She also claimed there was a swastika chalked on the floor of the service elevator.

As bizarre and preposterous as these charges seemed, I was duty-bound to investigate them. I have never been so reluctant to meet with anyone as I was when I entered my boss' office the following morning. He burst out laughing after I finished reading the accusation. "Are you kidding?" he almost shouted. I explained I needed a serious response for the record. He emphatically denied the allegation, and said he hadn't even spoken to the

"Fudge"

temp, much less hurled racial insults at her. Subsequent interviews with others confirmed this.

Later that afternoon I walked down the hallway leading to the service elevator to check out the second allegation. Apparently the swastika had been a sand mandala that had blown away in the night. There was no sign anything had ever been scrawled on the cement floor.

I filed my report with the EEO Office, concluding there was no basis for the charges, and quickly got on the phone. "Please come back to work," I begged the secretary on maternity leave. "You can bring the baby."

Mercifully, and for reasons of her own, the secretary did return to work early.

In the time between working for JV Equipment Company, and the State of California, Jim and I got married. Neither of us thought this would be legally possible just a year after I arrived in California.

Among the utility bills I'd retrieved from the mailbox early one Saturday morning, was an over-sized manila envelope. It was addressed to me, and postmarked Roanoke, Virginia. Jim sat across from me at the kitchen table when I opened it. I pulled out two sheets of legal-size paper stapled together. There were a couple of numbers at the top of the first page and the words "VIRGINIA. In the Hustings court for the city of Roanoke . . ." I continued reading. It was a divorce decree. I had no warning the divorce was even in progress.

"I'll go get a bottle of wine," Jim said, "and we'll have a toast." While he was gone I re-read the decree. I smiled as I read the words on the first page ". . . that the parties hereto are members of the Caucasian race." Frank was still in denial.

How ironic, I couldn't get a legal separation *in person*, in England—but could be divorced, *by mail*, in the United States.

Five months later Jim and I were married in a simple civil ceremony in Carson City, Nevada.

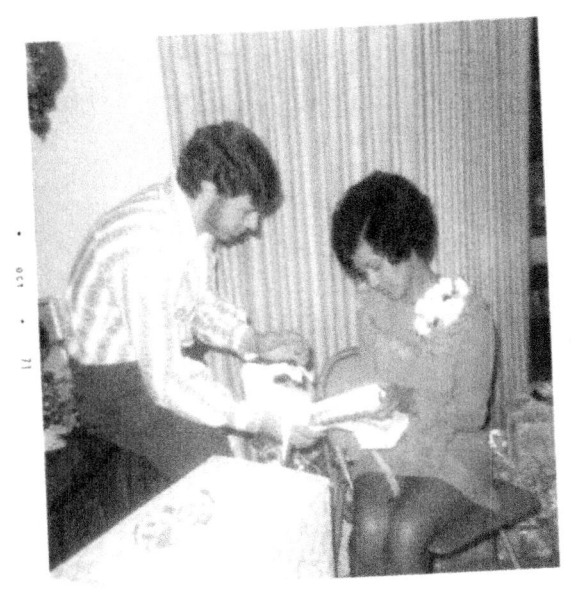

Our wedding reception at Jim's parents' home
Sacramento, California-1971

On the cover of the Department of
Water Resources' employee magazine
The California State Fair, Sacramento

Achieving a life-long goal: California State University, Sacramento, 1985

Tina (center), and Alicia, being sworn in as attorneys by Judge Ronald B. Robie

Sacramento December 1, 1998

HELLO AND GOODBYE

"We have a file on you."

I must have looked as stunned as I felt because his face softened.

"We were alerted that you were in the United States, and unable to support yourself, which, as you know, is a requirement for residency."

That's why Frank wanted to know where I lived when I first came over here. He was trying to get me deported.

I'd stared at the middle-aged man in a suit and tie who'd sat across from me in a spacious office in the John E. Moss Federal Building. I didn't know what was coming next.

Were they going to deport me? How could they, I'm married to an American.

"The contact was made eight years ago, so you can see you weren't exactly a high-priority case."

The official had smiled, closed the manila folder, and told me to continue my citizenship process.

A few months later, in a crowded Federal building conference room, I raised my hand and pledged allegiance to the United States of America. I wanted to become an American citizen so that I could vote. Twenty-nine years later I would vote for a man of my same racial mix—Barack Obama—who would become the 44th President of the United States.

"Fudge"

The same year I became a citizen I went back to England for a visit. It had been nine years since I'd left home to join Jim in Sacramento.

The flight was uneventful and Mother and Sid were clearly pleased to see all of us—I'd brought along Dean and Tina, who were 15-and 16-year-old teenagers, and Dean's girlfriend, Julie.

The inside of Mother's house looked freshly painted, and I could tell she had recently wall-papered the bedroom we were staying in. Malcolm was away at college so we had Mother's undivided attention—a rare treat. I enjoyed being part of Mother and Sid's daily routine. I was still in bed when I'd hear Sid whistling downstairs. Each morning he'd turn on the gas fire, which long ago replaced the open coal fire in the living room. The room would be warm when the rest of us tumbled out of bed. I'd hear Sid's cheerful greeting to the two milkmen as he welcomed them into the kitchen for a cup of tea. After the milkmen left, Sid would climb the stairs balancing a filled cup of steaming tea—Mother's morning treat in bed. The click of a lighter signaled Mother was having her cigarette, a sound I'd heard long before the sun rose.

Although Sid's accounting job at the Whitworth's mill was at least a 10-mile round trip, he came home each noontime. Mother had his food on the table like clockwork. One dinner time, she paced from the kitchen, where the food was cooling, to the living room, to check the clock on the mantelpiece. Sid was late. When he entered the back door, his glasses fogged up, and his face flushed from the long bike ride, Mother gave him "the look." Sid feigned annoyance at being chastised for being ten minutes late.

"I had the wind against me," he explained. But their eyes had met and they smiled.

My month-long visit home was filled with nostalgic moments. If it wasn't Sid who woke me, it would be the next-door-neighbor, Derrick Minter. His still-vibrant whistling brought back girlhood memories.

There were times Derrick would be leaving out of his front gate, at the same time I was coming in mine. He'd greet me with a big broad grin, give me a wink and one of his cheery, "Hello darlin', looking lovely," regardless of my appearance. His flattering words always made me smile, and gave me—an insecure teenager—a much-needed confidence boost.

Derrick was good-looking with a strong build, and a head of thick, dark hair. He had a wife, Eunice, and a bunch of kids—at least five. I'm not sure if Derrick ever had a regular job. Mother said the kids wouldn't recognize meat unless it was a rabbit—a testament to Derrick's successful hunting expeditions. Derrick could be seen flying around town on the golden wings of his huge BMW motorbike. You'd think he didn't have a care in the world, which was quite a contrast from his wife who looked perpetually tired.

On weekends the Minter's yard was filled with leather-jacketed lads smoking, laughing, and poking their motorbikes with one tool or another. On windy days the doors of Derrick's big garden hut, which stood a few feet from his back door, and faced ours, would bang open exposing his photo gallery of girls in various stages of undress. I was in my early teens then, and would stand on my tiptoes to get a better look. I marveled at the breasts of some of those girls. They looked like beach balls about to pop. I realized I had a *very* long way to go.

There were times when Derrick would come roaring up behind me as I tottered back from town on my stiletto heels.

"Want a lift, love?" he'd shout above the sound of his duel exhausts. I'd tug my tight skirt above the line of decency, and attempt to mount the rumbling vehicle. Even though we were only a street away from our house, I was completely transformed by the time we arrived. My hair, which had been backcombed to a height of several feet, and sprayed stiff with lacquer for good measure, was now a three foot ducktail sticking off the back of my head. When I dismounted, my skirt, which had barely cooperated in the effort to hoist it to a length where I could straddle the bike, was stuck to my thighs and refused to budge. I'm sure all the nosy neighbors got a good laugh when they saw me.

"Sid said it must have been the English air," wrote my mother three months after I returned to the States. She was responding to the news I was pregnant. The pregnancy was a shock to Jim and me. We'd been married for nine years, and no baby. I was thirty-five, considered old for being pregnant then, and had two teenagers, so I was conflicted. I'd been raising children since I was eighteen and looking forward to some freedom. At the same, I loved all phases of raising Dean and Tina. Jim was overjoyed I was pregnant. He'd raised my children as his own, but they were five and six years old when we'd met. Now he'd have the pleasure of raising his child from infancy. Jim was a nurturing person, and I knew he'd help with the baby. I was right. When the baby boy we named Aaron, cried, Jim almost tackled me to reach him first.

Three months after we celebrated Aaron's first birthday, October 1981, I was awakened by a telephone call at two o'clock in the morning. I wasn't alarmed by the early morning call—Mother often forgot England was eight hours ahead of California. In a voice choked with tears, she eventually managed to get the words out. My brother, Terry, who'd immigrated to Adelaide, in South Australia a decade earlier, was dead. He'd committed suicide by taking an overdose of pills.

I could hardly believe my ears. Terry was only 39. Little, by little, Mother sobbed out the details. She knew Terry was having problems. He'd told Mother his wife was divorcing him, and that he wasn't allowed to see his two sons.

"Terry told me he was thinking about coming home. I told him he was better off staying in Australia." I could hear the anguish in her voice.

Mother, ever the pragmatist, had told him there was still no work in England—the reason Terry had immigrated to Australia.

Mother blamed Terry's wife for his death, although she knew little about their marital situation. She threatened to go to Australia and "sweep the floor with her." It was an idle threat, if ever there was one. Mother hated to travel. A taxi downtown to play bingo was as far as she'd go. I couldn't imagine her flying for 20 hours to get to Australia.

Although Terry and I were not close, we wrote to each other when I was living in California and he'd moved to Australia. We exchanged photographs of our growing children. Terry had two sons, Clive and Mark. I'd smiled when I looked at one of the Polaroid photographs he'd sent. There was Terry standing in a swimming pool, burned brown from the Australian sun. He looked a lot different from the pasty-faced kid I'd grown up with.

The news of Terry's death triggered memories of our childhood. He was the one mistreated the most by the

"Fudge"

Old Man. The abuse had an effect on Terry. He was withdrawn—a sad, angry kid with few friends. He showed little enthusiasm for anything, except the Army Cadets, a military youth organization.

Terry would spend hours preparing his uniform for the Cadet meetings. He'd whiten his military belt with Blanco—a cake-like compound soldiers used. He'd cadge Mother's liquid Brasso to shine the buckle on his belt, and the badges on his beret. Terry's face would brighten from sullen to proud whenever he pulled on his thick woolen army trousers and jacket, buckled up his belt and donned his beret ready to march in the town's annual parade. He'd hold his head high as he kept perfect time to the beat of the marching band.

When Terry telephoned Mother from Australia and told her he was thinking about returning to England, perhaps all he needed to hear was he *could* come home—that he was wanted, and welcome.

Terry with sons Clive (left), Mark (rear), and a friend.

Australia 1976

DO NOT BEND

Mother's pale blue airmail envelopes were always crammed with family news, some good, but a lot bad, and sad. I think it helped her to write things down. When I carefully opened one of her letters—and I had to open them all carefully because Mother wrote on every available square inch and I could accidentally tear off some words—I thought I was going to read some good news. She'd told me in an earlier letter the Council was preparing to renovate her house. They'd moved her down the street while the work was being done.

Most people would look forward to having an indoor toilet and central heat after living in a house without either for thirty-five years, but not Mother. I could just see her sitting in the strange temporary house the Council had provided, pouring her heart out in her letter to me.

> *"Pauline there were so many memories there I did not want it to be done, but it is a government ruling now they all have to be done and the day they started on it I went up and there in the yard was our bath broken in half, the back door off, the kitchen window gone it was just like a barn, it nearly killed me. I was heartbroken."*

I realized, for the first time, just how traumatic change

was for my mother. Her life-long mantra, "Better the hell you know, than the hell you don't know," extended beyond the trap which tied her to the Old Man for years. Any upheavals—even a beneficial one—were distressing to her.

Mother did adjust. Now she had an indoor bathroom, upstairs in what was once the boys' back bedroom. The dreaded outside toilet was gone, as was the room with the bathtub where our Irish lodger, Gus, scalded his legs. Gone, too, was the dark coal hole where the coalmen dumped hundred weight sacks of coal and inhaled a cloud of poisonous coal dust. Mother had radiators providing central heat to keep her warm—no need anymore to fill the rubber hot water bottles each night.

When the words, "Photos Do not Bend," were scrawled on the outside of Mother's padded brown envelopes, I knew I'd be treated to yet more Polaroid pictures of the inside of her posh new home. I was happy for her.

A few years later Mother would have reason to show off again. She and Sid purchased their house from the Council. This was an option the Council allowed all their tenants and was, by all accounts, an excellent deal. Like others in the neighborhood who had bought their homes, Mother immediately made changes to the outside to distinguish it from the rental houses.

All the old-fashioned sash windows were changed to a more modern style. White paint replaced the exterior green color. The rickety wooden front fence was replaced with brick, and the slat gate to black wrought iron. Subsequent photographs showed an enclosed front porch built onto the front of the house, courtesy of my brother Kevan, and his son, Jason. At long last Mother would have a barrier from the icy winter blasts which slammed doors, and sucked out any heat the fire had generated.

PART FIVE

Family Matters

I WANDER LONELY

In addition to letters from Mother, I'd get the occasional letter from my eldest sister, Sheila. I knew she didn't have much money, although I was never sure why. Her husband, Pete, always had a job. When I was fifteen, he was employed by the local Council as a dustman. I was enough of a snob to be embarrassed when Pete shouted my name while hanging on the back of the moving ash cart, as it drove passed me and a girlfriend. Sheila had no such false pride. She'd cross the street to my Mother's house and proudly show the family the nice clothes the wealthy people had tossed out, and Pete had brought home. Nobody said anything to Sheila, but none of us would've been seen dead in those clothes.

I'd send Sheila a Christmas card each year and slip in a couple of dollars. She always wrote and thanked me. In 1985, when I was living in California, Sheila may have opened one of my cards just a few days before her husband, Pete, died. He passed away from stomach cancer on Christmas Eve.

When Sheila and I wrote to each other we shared superficial news. I had to wait for Mother's letters to get the details of Sheila's tumultuous life. I felt sorry for her when I read these accounts. She and I got along well when we were kids, probably because we stuck out like sore thumbs—Sheila with her one arm, and me with brown skin and frizzy hair.

Mother often paired us together. I was the kid Mother told to travel with Sheila to get her fitted for her first artificial arm. We travelled by train to Roehampton, in Southwest London, to a facility previously used to provide prosthetics for disabled soldiers. It was a two-hour trip—a long way for two country kids in their early teens that never went anywhere. Neither Mother, nor the Old Man, bothered to come with us.

Sheila's artificial arm was made of a heavy plastic. It was designed so her partial right arm nestled into a hollowed-out section of the prosthetic. Thick straps were connected to the artificial arm and worn across Sheila's shoulder. The hand, which looked like one you'd find on a mannequin, had stationary curled fingers, and a movable thumb. When Sheila reached forward, the strap mechanism pulled the thumb upward which enabled her to grasp the handle of her bag—or something similar. My sister didn't wear the prosthesis very often—it was heavy, and looked unsightly unless it was worn with long sleeves. Besides, Sheila was able to do everything a two-armed person could do, and better than some.

A John Lea School sewing teacher grabbed my arm as I hurried out of the sewing class one afternoon. "You should be ashamed of your sloppy work," she said. "Your sister, who only has one arm, sews so much better than you do with two." It was true.

At home I'd sit next to Sheila by the bay window in the living room. Her short right arm would act as a stand supporting a lacy white tablecloth, and I'd watch as she patiently embroidered crinoline ladies with their parasols, using a rainbow of silken threads. Sheila would also use her short arm as a darning mushroom. She'd slip the worn heel of a sock over the arm, and weave the woolen thread with her left hand until the hole was invisible. Sheila became adept at carrying a variety of things in the arm's spongy crevice. Her lit cigarette drew the most attention.

Sometimes Sheila would take me to visit her best friend, Barbara Cox, who lived in the Kingsway Estate on the other side of Croyland Park. One particular night we were walking arm-in-arm toward her friend's house. Sheila was quietly reciting one of our favorite poems, "Daffodils," by William Wordsworth.

I wandered lonely as a cloud
That floats on high o'er vales and hills,
When all at once I saw a crowd,
A host, of golden daffodils;
Beside the lake, beneath the trees,
Fluttering and dancing in the breeze.

Sheila's voice was the only sound I could hear. There were no blaring wirelesses or televisions. The silence gave me an eerie feeling. When we arrived at Barbara's house we learned why the estate was so quiet. The BBC had cancelled all programs except for news bulletins. King George VI had died. He'd passed away from lung cancer at the age 56. He, and his Queen, Elizabeth, were beloved by the British people and became even more popular when they refused to be evacuated out of London during the German bombing in World War II. Sixteen months later, mourning turned to celebration in every town and village in the country when the King's 25-year-old daughter, Elizabeth, was driven in an eight horse-drawn golden coach to be crowned Queen in Westminster Abbey on June 2, 1953.

Pete was Sheila's first boyfriend. She was 16 when they met—he was about ten years older.

"He's nice looking," Sheila confided to me one evening as we stood warming our hands by the living room fire. "He has blond hair and blue eyes."

Sheila was all smiles as she shared her secret with me. Not long after, Pete gave her a ring. Unfortunately, they spent more time falling out rather than falling in love. More than one night, my brothers and sisters, and I, would press our noses against the upstairs window to watch Pete searching our front garden with a flashlight. Sheila had thrown her engagement ring at him, yet again, after one of their fierce arguments. During a lull in their battles, they headed for the Registry Office and were married. Two of their three children, Donna and Richard, were born during the following four years. A third child, Matthew was born much later.

Donna and Richard looked angelic with their mass of golden hair—the same color as their father's. Donna was such a beautiful child neighbors would suggest to Sheila she enter her baby in the Miss Pears Baby Soap Contest. I don't think she did. We didn't talk about such things, but I imagine Sheila was relieved to have children who were not disabled, and would never suffer the verbal abuse hurled at her.

"One-arm Jimmy" and "peg leg," were two names often hurled at Sheila as she and I strolled down the street, minding our own business. I knew what it was like to be attacked without provocation.

I'd be skipping along the street, daydreaming as usual, when someone would call out, "Blackie," or "Nigger."

When I'd hear one of those names, I'd turn to confront some spiteful kid. Once in a while it wasn't a kid at all, but an adult calling out for their black dog. With all the millions of names to choose from, I couldn't understand why people would choose names like these for their animals.

Sheila and her family moved into a council house directly across the street from Mother. Too close, in Mother's opinion. It was impossible for her not to hear the arguments which spilled out into the street. As much as Mother wanted to stay out of their lives, there were times when she felt compelled to intervene.

"I had to phone Kevan to look for Sheila the other night," Mother once wrote. "She ran out of her house in the cold without a coat or shoes. They're always fighting, it's driving me crazy."

Mother's letters described situations far beyond a couple having an occasional argument. Sheila was deteriorating mentally and emotionally.

"They gave her that shock treatment," Mother wrote, "it didn't do any good. I think it made her worse."

I knew what Mother was talking about. I'd seen the movie, "One Flew over the Cuckoo's Nest." I'd read that shock therapy was designed to induce seizures to reconnect nerves, and lift depression—but it was considered controversial. I was thankful I'd moved thousands of miles away after reading letters like these.

Sheila in her early twenties

Sheila and Pete on their
wedding day
Wellingborough, 1959

DORIS AND SID

Many of Mother's letters included a description of her ailments. This was not hypochondria. Mother suffered with a variety of bronchial conditions which her heavy smoking didn't help, and probably caused. She also had frequent headaches. I would often come home from school to find her sitting in a chair, bent over with her head in her hands. A small round tin was never far away from her, filled with codeine tablets which could be purchased over the counter at Boots Chemist. None of us knew codeine was a narcotic, and addictive.

I was used to hearing about mother's ailments, and was surprised when one of her letters talked about Sid.

"He's had two heart strains," she wrote.

Sid's heart problems were serious enough he couldn't ride his bike to work, and the company sent a car for him.

Someone else must have broken the news to me. I know Mother wouldn't have been able to speak to tell me what happened.

Both Sid and Malcolm enjoyed a pint, or more. They had a Friday night ritual where they'd walk arm-in-arm to the Star Public House, about a mile from home. On one of those evenings, as they turned the corner from Henshaw Road on to Croyland Road, just the red post box, Sid dropped to his knees. Malcolm held onto his dad, screaming for help. Sid died in the hospital a few hours later from a massive heart attack.

When I heard Sid had died, I was so thankful I'd been home the year before when Jim and I brought our five-year-old son, Aaron, back to England for a visit. I was glad too, Jim had treated Mother, Sid, and Malcolm to dinner at the Hind Hotel—one of the most elegant places to eat at the time. Mother had written she and Sid talked about the dinner for months.

I thought how much Mother would miss Sid. How she'd miss the playful banter she'd described in her letters.

"Sid loves the wool hat with the ear flaps you sent him. I have to make him take it off when he's having his dinner," Mother wrote.

"Sid bought me some earrings to match the pearl necklace you sent me. He said now he definitely has to insure me."

I flew home for Sid's funeral. My sole recollection of the event was of Malcolm chastising my sister, Delly, and me for laughing at something or other as we talked about what we'd wear to the service. We were both insensitive—not fully understanding the depth of Malcolm's grief.

Doris didn't attend the funeral. She was living in the U.S., but even if she'd been in England she may not have attended. Doris and Sid never got along. She blamed him for Mother's separation from the Old man, and thought Sid was stingy with his money. I didn't realize how strongly she disliked Sid until I saw Doris' wedding photographs. She'd chosen our brother, Terry, to give her away.

In a phone call after I returned to the States, Mother

told me where she and Malcolm scattered Sid's ashes.

Sid liked to go rabbit hunting. He kept several pet ferrets in a hutch in the back yard. He'd hold them and pet them. Everyone else thought they were vicious little creatures ready to bite off a finger or two, given the chance. Sid's rabbiting expeditions involved hauling the writhing ferrets in a sack to a rabbit burrow, releasing them to flush out the rabbits, whereupon Sid, and the rest of the big game hunters, would shoot the rabbits as they bolted from the holes. The ferrets would be scooped back in the sack to hunt another day.

"I thought Sid would want me to scatter his ashes in the field where he liked to go rabbiting," Mother told me over the phone, bright and early one morning. I cried, picturing my mother, arm-in-arm with her blind son, fumbling their way through some wet, weed-filled field, scattering the ashes of their beloved Sid.

I'd been surprised by Sid's death, but a few years later I got even more shocking news. My sister, Doris, at age forty-seven, had died from a cerebral hemorrhage. Between wrenching sobs, Mother was able to give me the details.

"Willie phoned me and said Doris was in the hospital. He knew something was wrong when she told him her head hurt so much she wasn't going to work. You know Doris. She never missed a day."

"I remember," I said, "she was always a hard worker." I could hear my mother's voice cracking.

"Willie gave her a couple of tablets but they didn't help. Doris collapsed when she tried to drag herself out of bed to go to the lavatory. They rushed her to the hospital and said she'd had a stroke. When I got to the hospital, Willie told me Doris was feeling a bit better, but when I saw her she looked awful—one side of her face was all droopy. The nurses told her to stay down, but she wouldn't listen, and tried to get out of bed. She had another stroke." Mother started sobbing again.

"I'm so sorry, Mum," I said. I was sorry. Sorry my mother was hurting, and sorry she'd lost a daughter.

Doris and I had a miserable relationship during most of her life. She tormented me with cruel remarks about my appearance for as long as I can remember. She made no secret of the fact that she was ashamed to be related to me. After we were both married the insults stopped, and she was always affectionate and attentive to my children. But the damage was done. I felt nothing during the conversation with my grieving mother. It's as if she was talking about a stranger. My eyes were dry.

"GOODBYE LOVE, NO ONE'S LEAVING"

The phone rang. Another call before daybreak.

"Crumbs," I'd grumbled to my husband's back, "After twenty-five years you'd think Mother would remember the time difference."

"Hello," I said without lifting my head off the pillow.

"Hello, Pauline?"

My mother coughed the question into the phone. I wasn't sure what other woman she expected to answer the phone at 2:00 a.m., 10:00 a.m. British time. I could hear her wheezing, louder than usual.

"Mum, you sound terrible."

"I can't get rid of this damn thing," she said.

"Have you been to the doctor?"

"Those twits don't know what they're doing. It's this sodding weather. It's been bitterly cold, and the rain hasn't let up for weeks."

Typical British weather. God, that's one thing I don't miss.

Mother had a perpetual cough, and suffered with a bout of bronchitis every year. She'd smoked since she was a kid in Ireland, but quit once when her "quack" told her to. It lasted a week. I was fully awake now, so I shifted to a sitting position, and we'd chat back and forth about one family member or another.

"Take care of yourself, Mum," I'd said, "Please see a

doctor."

It was the last time I talked with my mother. She died a week later of emphysema.

When I'd grumbled to my husband each time Mother woke me up in the wee hours, he'd predict one day I would miss those calls. He was right.

"I'm going home for Nan's funeral," I told my son, Dean, over the phone. He was an eight-hour drive away, attending Graduate school in Santa Barbara. "Jim is staying here with Aaron. We didn't think it was a good idea to leave a teenager alone. Tina cried when she told me she wished she could come with me. I told her I understood. I wouldn't want her to leave Cameron—he's just a year old."

"I'll come with you," was Dean's quiet response.

In the years since I first left England, it wasn't only the long flight which made me hesitant to go back. I found it heart-wrenching to leave each time. Both Mother and I would start crying the night before I was to return to the States. I'd start crying again in the morning, and continued until I arrived at the airport. Each time I left I thought it would be the last time I'd see my Mother, and one day it was. Although leaving home was painful, I was glad I returned once in a while. None of the children in our family ever got any physical affection from Mother, or the Old Man. Coming home gave me an excuse to put my arms around my mother when we greeted each other, and again when we said goodbye.

Takeoffs and landings scared me the most, and it helped to have Dean with me. I enjoyed my son's company. He's an avid reader, interested in a variety of things, and has a great sense of humor. Our conversations during the long flight distracted me from my grief.

Dean was still single at 31, although he was never

"Fudge"

without a girlfriend. He was currently with a young woman, Lyn, who he'd been seeing on, and off, for nine years. He enjoyed his life, and obviously wasn't in any hurry to get married. He had an under-graduate degree in electronic engineering, and had worked in Japan for Sony Corporation. He spoke Japanese, which amazed me—it seemed like a difficult language to learn.

Some people said Dean looked like me, but I didn't see the resemblance. If you didn't know I was Dean's mother, you'd think his ethnicity was middle-eastern. His skin is fair, his features small, his black hair—spared my frizz—sat neatly on his head in soft waves. In the 1980s, when anyone who looked Iranian was considered a prospective hijacker, Dean said he often got dirty looks when he boarded a plane. One time, an airline official took away his passport and held it for four hours—leaving Dean just sitting there. When the official returned Dean asked, "What's the problem?"

"You don't want to know," was the cryptic response.

As the pilot announced our descent into London's Heathrow Airport, I fumbled for my passport. I'd been a U.S. citizen for sixteen years, but it still felt odd to travel on an American passport, and know I'd be considered a foreigner whenever I flew into London. I pulled out a narrow strip of paper along with my passport. It was Mother's obituary. I read it once again:

"Peacefully on Sunday, January 15th 1995, Elizabeth Mary, age 77 years. . ."

"Peacefully," it read. Mother was constantly calling out for peace.

"Will ye whisht," she would shout out to us noisy kids. "Give me some peace."

A short ride on the London tube from Heathrow Airport took us to the familiar St. Pancras train station. A little over an hour later we lugged our suitcases into the High View Hotel on Midland Road. A short taxi ride through the center of town brought us to the curb outside Mother's house. I was filled with dread. How would I be able to walk into my mother's house knowing she wouldn't be there to greet me at the doorway? She would never greet me anywhere, ever again.

My sister, Delly, who'd also flown in from California, opened the front door. We clung to each other, sobbing.

Delly was the youngest child of Mother and the Old Man, and was six years my junior. She and Doris looked alike when they were little—pretty kids with fair curly hair. When she was a child, Delly's hair was a tangled mess when she got up in the morning. It was my job to brush it. She would scream bloody murder. At times I would give up, which meant the next day her curls would be more matted, and harder to brush. If either parent was within earshot when she screamed, I would get a clout because I made her cry. This was in addition to the kick in the shins from Delly as she tried to make her escape from me. I still have the scar on my right leg.

Like my sister, Doris, and I, Delly married an American airman. She, and her husband Mike, had three children: Rachael, Wendy, and Michael. Unlike me, Delly had no fear of flying, and after she went to live in the U.S., she'd return to England to visit every year or so.

During a couple of her visits, after Mother was widowed, Delly would drive Mother and Malcolm to the seaside for a short holiday. I knew my mother agreed to this for Malcolm's benefit because she didn't like to travel. Delly telephoned me after she returned to the

States following one of her visits.

"After I got mum tucked away in the back seat of the rental car, and Malcolm settled in the front, I looked in the rear-view mirror before pulling away from the curb. Mother was already asleep with her mouth open."

I laughed, and told Delly, "I can only imagine how the rest of the holiday went."

As Dean and I entered Mother's living room, Malcolm got up from the couch.

"Hello, Pauline," he said, and attempted a smile.

I was overwhelmed with sadness. It was hard for me to breathe. Poor Malcolm. He and Mother were constant companions after Sid died. What would he do now that Mother had passed away? She'd waited hand-and-foot on Malcolm after he came home from college. As far as I knew, he didn't even know how to make himself a cup of tea.

Malcolm greeted me with a hug, and then stuck out his hand for Dean to shake. He backed up a few steps until he felt the edge of the couch against his legs, and then lowered himself down. Delly settled into Mother's favorite easy chair by the bay window. It gave me an eerie feeling to see her sitting there, cigarette in hand, legs tucked beneath her, just like Mother did.

The funeral service was to be held at Our Lady's Roman Catholic Church on Ranelagh Road—the church we made infrequent visits to when we were kids—and the one my mother never set foot in. My brother Kevan, was taking care of the details.

Although Mother wouldn't have admitted it, I think Kevan was her favorite of the Old Man's kids. And not because he looked the most like his father—something I would never point out to him.

"You're all the same to me," Mother used to say when someone was accused of being her "pet."

Kevan may have inherited the Old Man's looks, but he didn't inherit his disposition. Kevan was easygoing and quick to laugh. He and Terry were often sent out on errands together. Saturday was market day, and the Old Man would order my brothers to go downtown to scrounge empty wooden orange crates from the fruit sellers. The crates were chopped and used for firewood when we couldn't afford coal. The boys would load the crates, and any fruit they could cadge, into an old baby pram to haul home. The pram came in handy for other things too.

When Mother didn't have enough money to have the coal delivered to the house, she'd have Kevan and Terry push the pram a couple of miles to the coal depot at the railway station on Midland Road. They were told to buy a few shillings worth of coal, which was still a heavy load for two young boys. Kevan told me years later he and Terry would swipe the coal when the coalmen were having their tea break, and spend the money on sweets.

Kevan may have had other girlfriends but he only brought Heather to the house. She was an only child—a pretty girl from a nice family who lived in Finedon, a village not far from us. Several years after Kevan and Heather married, Mother shared some good news in a letter.

"...I am so glad for him I had nearly given up hope, but when he rang one dinner-time and told me Heather was expecting I dropped everything I had in my hand."

It must have been a welcome feeling for Mother to be excited about the birth of a baby, something missing with her own pregnancies. Heather gave birth to a son, Jason,

"Fudge"

and a few years later, another baby boy they named Asa.

Dean and I barely spoke as we sat at the High View's breakfast table and devoured the English breakfast of bacon, eggs, sausage, fried tomatoes, and crumpets—washed down with cups of tea. We were well fortified for our walk to the John Drage Funeral Home on Croyland Road. The large, gleaming, brass nameplate mounted on the brick building by the front entrance, looked the same as I remembered it. As a child, I'd raced by the building knowing what was inside. After Dean and I identified ourselves the funeral director led us into the waiting room.

"I was told yesterday there wouldn't be a viewing. The body hasn't been prepared," he said apologetically. Both Delly and I had told Kevan we didn't want to see Mother. I'd changed my mind—telling Dean the night before that Mother would be upset if she knew I had come all this way, and hadn't stopped in to see her. "I could imagine Mother saying, 'Pauline, I'll give you a thump if you don't come and see me.'"

As I approached the casket I began to regret my decision. I was afraid of what Mother would look like dead. It had been nine years since I'd seen her alive. I held on to Dean's arm as I looked down at the stiff, lifeless body and searched for something I recognized. Mother looked like a grey manikin. Her fingernails were black. I touched her, and we left.

"Dean and I plan to walk to the church since it's so close to our hotel," I told Kevan and Delly. We were sipping tea at Mother's kitchen table. Dean and Malcolm were in the living room talking politics. Delly frowned. "Don't you think you should ride in the funeral car with us?" she said.

No, I thought, but didn't say. Mother had lived her whole life without regard to convention so I doubted she would disapprove.

"We're so close to the church," I reiterated, "it seems silly to come all the way across town, and then go back to where we just left."

Delly dropped the subject.

We talked about who might be at the funeral. My eldest brother, Terry, died 14 years earlier at age 39, in Australia; Doris, passed away 4 years earlier, aged 47, in the same wintry month of January as Mother. Sid had died almost a decade earlier. Besides the three of us in the kitchen, and Dean and Malcolm, we assumed Sheila, Eileen, and Billy would be there. Doris' widower, Willie, and their daughter, Tara, were also expected.

We were worried about Sheila. She'd been mentally ill for a number of years, and her behavior was unpredictable. Kevan recalled when Sheila attended Doris' funeral.

"On a freezing cold January day, Sheila showed up wearing a thin dress, and carpet slippers," he'd said.

Nobody at the table said anything.

"But at least she showed up," Kevan said.

This was more than I did.

Bundled up against the cold, Dean and I strolled back to the hotel, arm-in-arm. When we reached the corner of Croyland Road, I pointed across the street at the red post box.

"That's where Sid collapsed from a heart attack."

I tightened my headscarf, and lowered my head against the wind.

The next morning, Dean and I walked the short distance to Our Lady's Catholic Church, and joined Delly and the other family members in the front pews. Malcolm had written something to read. I'd watched him the day

"Fudge"

before writing in Braille—struggling to put his feelings into words.

After the priest finished the service, Kevan guided Malcolm to the church lectern. I was standing next to Delly, and as we were getting ready to sit down, she started to collapse. I couldn't hold her up. Dean, and my brother Billy, rushed to help me. They carried Delly outside. Dean, and my sister-in-law, Heather, stayed with Delly so Billy could return to the service. I was concerned about Delly, and my attention drifted away from Malcolm's heartfelt tribute.

At the graveside, Delly started to crumble again. As soon as I felt her slipping I whispered to her, "Delly, pull yourself together. Mother wouldn't want this kind of public display." She clung even tighter to my arm, but managed to stay on her feet.

My childhood friend, Dawn, was at the gravesite. Kevan said he'd seen her at a couple of our other family funerals. I'd wished I'd lived closer so I could have been there for her when her mother died. Mrs. Baker had been so good to me over the years. "She loved you, you know," Dawn once told me.

As we stood in the chilling wind and rain, I searched the faces of two elderly mourners, their features partially obscured by their hooded headscarves knotted tightly under their chins. Was it Mrs. Thompson who once lived across the street from Mother? Was she Sylve Evans, the barmaid Mother thought had her eye on Sid for years? I'd been gone for too long, and I couldn't tell.

Mother was laid to rest next to my sister Doris' grave. After the burial the mourners made their way back to Mother's house for refreshments. I was relieved to get in from the cold, even though the air was blue from all the smokers. Doris' husband, Willie, and their daughter, Tara, who I had never met, were among the group crowded into the small living room. As Dean and I entered the room I noticed Willie looked at my son, then at me, and then gave a knowing glance over to his daughter. Perhaps it was my paranoia, but the glance said to me, "This is the half-black sister I told you about." I thought back to the day when he'd sent Doris to the bus stop to make sure I didn't come to his house and embarrass him in front of his air force supervisor.

I exchanged a few words with Willie and his daughter as I made my way through the smoke to the bay window—Mother's favorite place to sit. Through the white lace curtains I watched as Sheila crossed the street from her house, and opened Mother's front gate. Soon after she entered the living room, she cadged a cigarette from someone, and proceeded to add to the air pollution. I tried to put on a neutral face when I looked at Sheila, but inside I was very sad.

Many of the thin blue airmail letters flying across the Atlantic from Mother's hand to mine would describe Sheila as being mentally and emotionally at rock bottom. Mother hadn't been exaggerating. Sheila looked a lot older than her 54 years. Her pale skin was dry and blotchy. Her hair was oily and uncombed, and her coat, and the dress underneath it, was stained, and too thin for the January cold.

Sixteen years would pass before Sheila and I would meet again, and neither of us would recognize the other.

I decided to visit Wellingborough for a few days on my way back to the U.S. from Italy. I'd agreed to accompany two friends on a European trip after one too many glasses of wine, which numbed my memory of miserable nine hour flights in blood-clot inducing cramped quarters. I was in for a surprise when I left the airport and arrived via the London underground to the train station for the 90-minute ride east to Wellingborough.

My memory of St Pancras Station was one of a dingy, smoky cavernous structure, suffering from decades of neglect. When St. Pancras first opened in 1868, it was described as, "... a masterpiece of Victorian Gothic Architecture..." and had the distinction of having the largest single-span roof in the world. Despite its deterioration, I was shocked to read, that in 1966, British Rail proposed to demolish it. Public outcry put a stop to that disastrous notion. St. Pancras was not only saved, but eventually became a destination station for the high-speed trains that zoomed back and forth under the English Channel, thereby justifying its renovation and expansion. It was reopened by the Queen in 2007.

I felt as if I had stumbled into a futuristic space station when I entered St. Pancras for the first time following its renovation. The entire place was spacious, bright and spotless, with soaring metal arches. Along with the structural improvements, an extensive avenue of boutiques, and trendy little cafés with gleaming glass fronts, had replaced the smoky dives and sooty walls. St. Pancras had regained its former glory. I thoroughly enjoyed roaming around the station, and was so busy admiring all the changes that I almost missed my train.

The October air was crisp, and the sky a bright blue, as I strolled from the Hind Hotel on Sheep Street where I was staying, to Sheila's house in Mannock Road. Many of the little brick council houses with their small square front gardens, privet hedges, and wooden front gates still looked presentable seven decades after they were built.

My mother's house was on the corner across from

Sheila's. The front area looked neat enough, but Mother's crimson wallflowers, and golden daffodils, were gone. I was standing outside Mother's house, lost in thought, when a small car, speeding up the road and careening around the corner, broke the silence. How full of life our street used to be—kids playing, men delivering everything from milk to coal, the clip clop of horse-drawn carts led by scruffy men calling out their wares, and my favorite sound—the chimes of the Walls' ice cream van that triggered my dash home to beg for money to buy a cornet, a wafer, or an ice lolly.

I crossed the street to Sheila's house, entered the front gate, took a few steps, and knocked on the front door.

A hand pulled back the net curtain at the front window and a face appeared. I didn't recognize it. The hair was short and mostly gray, and whiskers sprouted from the upper lip and the chin.

Sheila must have moved.

"'oo is it?" The face said loudly. It sounded like Sheila's voice.

"It's Pauline," I said.

"'oo?" was the reply.

"Pauline, your sister from America."

"Oh my God," the voice said flinging open the front door. It was only when I saw the missing right arm I knew for certain it was Sheila.

"Pauline, I never thought I would ever see you again. I know you won't believe this, but I dreamed you had come home."

Tears squirted from my eyes as I followed this stooped woman into the small living room. It was hard to believe she was only three years older than I was. We hugged each other and she offered me a chair—told me to find somewhere to sit without clothing piled on the seat.

"Fudge"

"Do you mind if I smoke?" she'd asked, deftly removing a cigarette from the packet with one hand.

I did mind, but I shook my head no. Sheila talked nonstop, jumping from one subject to another, and in between, expressing her amazement at seeing me. Somebody knocked on the front door.

"It's probably these men that are always after me. They won't leave me alone, Pauline. I don't want anything to do with them."

She shook her head in annoyance as she moved to the window. Sheila peered through the curtain and declared it was her home help lady.

"I'll tell her to f--k off."

I gasped. I hadn't heard profanity used so easily since before mother died.

"Please don't do that," I asked Sheila, "have her come in."

I heard Sheila tell the visitor her sister Pauline from America was visiting. An attractive dark-haired woman in her thirties appeared with a surprised look on her face. I was still having crying jags, and when Sheila told her how long it had been since we'd seen each other, the young woman became teary too. Her name was Alina Popowicz, one of several people who came each week to help Sheila.

Popowicz, that's a surname you'd never have heard in Wellingborough when I was growing up.

"I'll make you both a nice cup of tea," she offered, and bustled off to the kitchen.

She re-appeared with tea and sandwiches, gently inquiring if Sheila had taken her medication. My sister and I talked some more, and when I got up to leave, I asked Alina to walk with me to the gate. Sheila and I hugged at the front door.

"I'm so honored you came to see me," Sheila said, eliciting a burst of guilty tears from me. I'd been undecided about visiting her—worried she might be too unstable.

Outside the front gate, I asked Alina how Sheila was doing. Mother had written that Sheila was a paranoid schizophrenic, but I didn't know if that was an actual medical diagnosis, or Mother's opinion. Alina couldn't tell me anything more, citing privacy restrictions.

Alina told me how surprised she was to walk into Sheila's house and see me sitting there.

"You know when Sheila opened her front door and told me her sister from America was visiting, I thought she was having another episode. I almost fell over when I saw you sitting in the chair." We both laughed. Then she grew serious.

"Sheila panics when her son Matthew doesn't come to see her. She's convinced something terrible has happened, and she calls the police. They are used to this now and just talk to her, and reassure her Matthew is okay, perhaps just delayed."

I declined Alina's offer of a lift back to the hotel. I was looking forward to the walk. The air was colder, but it was still bright out. I pulled my wool scarf from around my neck and tied it around my head and set off.

I had no idea Sheila would be so happy to see me.

"Honored," she'd said that I'd taken the time to visit her. And to think I almost didn't go.

After most of the crowd that had gathered at Mother's house after the funeral had left, Dean and I pulled on our coats ready to leave. I declined Delly's offer to drive us back to our hotel—our walks had become therapeutic. When we reached the corner of Market and Sheep Streets, we turned into the Hind Hotel for a nightcap.

The hotel was built in the 1600's, and is Wellingbor-

"Fudge"

ough's architectural jewel. The grand Tudor-style coach inn occupies a central position facing the town's pedestrian Market Square. Above the arched columned entrance is a large wooden porch displaying a coat of arms, and supporting the imposing figure of a golden hind.

As Dean and I sat sipping our beer, I told him the history of my fascination with the hotel.

"My sister, Sheila, worked here as a chambermaid, along with her best friend, Barbara Cox. She'd tell me how she and Barbara were scared to death to clean the room with a hidden passage. As a kid, I'd only dare peer through the leaded glass windows, but I couldn't see much. The first time I stepped inside the Hind was when we brought mum, Sid and Malcolm here for dinner ten years ago. We'd talked about the secret passage during the meal, and Jim wanted to return to the hotel the next day so he could learn more.

The hotel manager was nice enough to show Jim and me around when we showed up at the reception desk the following afternoon. We followed him up the circular red-carpeted stairs to the second level. The floor was uneven, and we could hear it creaking. We stopped at a door marked, "The Cromwell Suites." The manager unlocked the door and led the way across a dimly-lit outer room, to an interior door on the far side. We entered the Oak Room, a smaller version of the outer room—floor-to-ceiling dark wood paneling with a beamed ceiling. I remember there were upholstered chairs arranged around a long table that filled most of the room. There were a few framed paintings on the walls, and one or two decorative metal plates propped on a ledge just below the ceiling. A small candelabrum was mounted on each side of the fireplace on the far wall.

Jim asked the manager to show him the secret passage. The guy gestured to Jim to take a look for himself. Jim walked slowly around the room, pressing the dark paneling. The three of us were smiling, enjoying the mystery. When Jim moved passed the fireplace he pressed the large panel that adjoined the side wall. I burst out laughing when he jumped back as the panel opened inward. He'd found the passage. Jim and I took turns stepping into the secret passage, taking care that one of us stood outside.

Back downstairs in Cromwell's bar, I shared the rest of the Hind's history with Dean.

"I did some research on the Hind when I got back to the States. I can't believe I didn't know this stuff when I was growing up here. Anyway, I learned that secret passages like the one upstairs are called 'Priest Holes.' It's where Catholic priests hid from the Protestant soldiers of Queen Elizabeth I. The story goes a hotel servant girl spied on a secret meeting between Cromwell and Sir Thomas Fairfax, one of his generals. They were planning the Battle of Naseby—which is a village just 10 minutes from here. The servant knew she'd been identified and hid in the secret passage. She was eventually discovered and killed. Legend has it her spirit still roams the hotel."

It was late, and there was nobody on duty to show Dean the secret passage, so we slipped quietly out through the hotel's revolving leaded glass front door, into the evening.

The flight back to California was as uneventful as the flight over. I thanked Dean for coming with me. It would've been a much more difficult trip without the comfort of his company.

There were so many questions I wish I'd been brave enough to ask my mother while she was alive. She was secretive when I was a child, but perhaps would've been more open as she grew older.

I was alone in my house in California on the first Saint Patrick's Day following Mother's death. I put on a CD by Irish tenor, Frank Patterson. I poured myself a glass of my favorite Chardonnay, raised a glass "to me mum," and joined Frank in singing, "I'll take you home again Kathleen."

The Hind Hotel

GONE FOR GOOD

I knew I'd have to phone first thing in the morning, California time, if I wanted to catch my brother, Malcolm, before he took off to the pub. The luminous green numbers on the oven clock read eight o'clock. *That makes it four in the afternoon in England.* I slid the carafe from its hot plate and poured myself a cup of coffee—if you could call it coffee since half the cup was hot milk.

Four decades ago when I arrived in California from England, I tried to drink my coffee black. That's how my husband drinks it, and it seemed the American thing to do—like my putting milk and sugar in tea was the British thing. I liked the idea of pouring that pungent, dark brown liquid into a mug and taking a swig, as cowboys do around a campfire. Well, I'm no cowboy, and coffee without milk tasted too bitter.

I drank coffee in England. Mother bought those small bottles of liquid Camp Coffee for me as a special treat. In my childish imagination I saw her gift as an acknowledgment of my American connection.

Camp Coffee was made in Scotland—initially produced for the military—easier to pour something than grind beans on the battlefield. The label on the bottle depicted a seated Gordon Highlander soldier holding a cup and saucer, with a Sikh servant standing next to him holding a tray. On a later version of the label, the Sikh was seated next to the kilted soldier drinking his own cup of coffee—a nod to the politically correct according to blogger Brian Edwards, a New Zealand writer: "An excellent example of racial equality and historical revisionism."

I was unaware of this controversy when I was in my teens, as I'd sit at the kitchen table, drinking my coffee and counting the cigarette burns on the oilcloth covering the table.

I dialed Malcolm's phone number, and smiled as I listened to the uniquely British double ring tone—brr brr, brr brr.

"Pauline, have you heard about Eileen?" Malcolm blurted out the question as soon as I said, "hello."

"Heard what? I said. He hadn't included the words, "the bad news" in his question, so I wasn't prepared.

"Eileen died."

"What?" I said, stupefied. "When? How?"

"A week ago. There were complications after she had leg surgery. I couldn't phone you earlier. You've never given me your new number."

Malcolm had few other details, and neither of us knew Eileen's home number.

"I'll call the international operator," I said before hanging up.

"Yes, it's true," said Steven, Eileen's long-time partner, responding to my disbelief. "Eileen tried to reach you when she went in for surgery, and I tried to find you when things took a turn for the worse."

I didn't know what to say to him. My sister was only 59 years old. Eileen was the one who'd first stopped writing, and we'd both moved and changed telephone numbers. She and I had always gotten along well, and

"Fudge"

we'd been writing more frequently in the decade since we'd seen each other at Mother's funeral. That is until she asked me for a loan.

"Can you lend me a couple of hundred, Pau?" she'd asked.

The furniture she and Steven had purchased was in danger of being repossessed. My answer was, "No. How are you going to pay me back if you can't afford your furniture payments?"

Eileen stopped writing. She didn't even send me a Christmas card. I thought I'd inoculated myself against the fickle affections of some of my family, but I hadn't. I was hurt. Months later I received a letter from Eileen. I didn't write back.

"How much did she really care about our relationship if she could cut me off over money for furniture?" I'd said to my husband, appealing for his support.

Jim was all about forgiving and moving on. I wasn't going to open myself up again. I remembered what happened with my sister, Doris. But now I was sorry I hadn't written back to Eileen. She didn't have Doris' personality, or her history of abuse toward me.

After I'd spoken with Steven, Eileen's companion, I'd reminisced with Jim.

"Eileen was a gentle soul when we were kids. She didn't participate in the name-calling, and physical fights which flared up among the rest of us at the slightest provocation."

"What are you smiling at?" my husband asked as we sat across from each other at the kitchen island on the uncomfortable wooden bar stools I regretted buying.

"I just remembered something that happened. I was 15, which meant Eileen was about 11 years old. Terry, Doris, and I were huddled around the coal fire in the living room one evening. We'd been trying to bribe each other to go to the shop for cigarettes, and chocolate. It was freezing outside and nobody wanted to leave the only warm room in the house. Eileen came in from the kitchen and volunteered to go. We pooled our money, wrote our wants on the corner of an envelope, and off she went. An icy blast blew in from outside as she left through the front door. We wouldn't see Eileen again for a couple of days. Mother must have called the police, but she told us nothing. The terrible thing was, none of us kids was worried about Eileen. We just wanted our stuff, or our money back. When Eileen eventually came home, she had neither."

"I remember you talking about Eileen," Jim said. "Isn't she the one who liked cats and old people?"

"Yes, she did, and she was always wandering off."

I can still hear Mother's voice. "Go and find Eileen. It's time for bed."

I grumbled out loud as I left the house—Mother's eyes boring a hole in the back of my head.

"Why do I always have to fetch Brick?"

All the kids in the family had a nickname, and "Brick" was Eileen's. I had no idea where the name came from, or what it meant. Eileen certainly wasn't shaped like a brick. She was the tallest kid in the family—taller even than our three brothers. She looked the most like Mother—thin frame, angular face, and grey eyes—and to my delight, her brown hair was frizzier than mine.

I'd learned from experience the first place to look for Eileen was at Lucy's, the cat woman's house. Lucy lived in a prefab on the hill near my friend Dawn. Unlike Dawn's well-lit home, Lucy's house was shrouded in darkness. The thick, velvet curtains covering the front windows constrained any signs of light. The house was surrounded by a garden of high weeds which provided ample cover for the herds of cats purported to be lurking there.

After I'd summoned enough courage to enter the garden gate, I'd sprint to the front steps, bang on the door, and then rush back down the path behind the safety of the gate. The door wouldn't open the first time I knocked, and I'd have to repeat the charge. Following my second attempt, Lucy would open the door a crack, and peer out. Her clothing was long, and dark, and her grey hair braided and pinned on top of her head. I was scared of Lucy. I'd seen her running up and down the street at night, calling for her cats—her unbound plaits a mass of wavy hair down to her waist. It was these episodes which served to cement her reputation as the neighborhood witch.

Eileen would emerge from the dimly-lit interior of Lucy's house after I shouted, "If you don't leave, Mum will come and get you, and she'll give you a clout."

Eileen knew this was no idle threat, having been thumped by Mother in the past for not coming when she was called. As Eileen and I sauntered arm-in-arm down Gilletts Road, I'd asked her why she kept going to Lucy's, and wasn't she scared. Eileen stopped walking and turned to face me.

"She didn't always look like she does now. I've seen photos of her when she was young—she was beautiful. Her husband's dead now, but he was an officer in the army, and they were stationed in India for a long time. They had a big house, and servants who wore turbans. She's told me lovely stories."

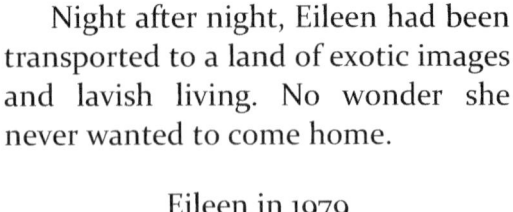

Night after night, Eileen had been transported to a land of exotic images and lavish living. No wonder she never wanted to come home.

Eileen in 1979
(Age 31)

In late June the same year after Eileen's death, an e-mail arrived from Eileen's adult daughter, my niece, Sarah. She and I had begun corresponding since her mother's death. I couldn't believe what I was reading. Sarah wrote my brother Malcom had died. *I'd only spoken to him on the phone the week before.*

Apparently Malcolm had dialed 999, the emergency number in England, to tell the operator he'd taken some pills. When the police arrived, Malcolm was able to open the front door, but then he collapsed. He died a month before his 50th birthday.

I struggled to understand what happened. I knew Malcolm had been laid off from his job at Barclays Bank several years ago. "He's got ever such a good job at Barclays Bank in Northampton transcribing dictation," Mother had written when Malcolm got the job after he'd graduated from college.

Northampton, the county town, was a twenty-minute bus ride away. The few times I'd come home, I enjoyed greeting Malcolm at the bus stop, and we'd walk arm-in-arm back to the house. Malcolm's years at the Sunshine Home for the Blind, and his subsequent college education, had transformed him from an uncontrollable brat to a mature, interesting companion, informed and well-spoken. He was a voracious reader, and The Royal National Institute for the Blind delivered stacks of huge Braille books to the house. He listened to the political broadcasts, and wasn't afraid to voice his opinion. Although he was compassionate about some things, he ranted and raved about the unemployed, "The Yobos and layabouts who go on the public dole as soon as they leave school are too lazy to get a job. If I, a blind man, can find work, why can't they?"

Unfortunately, Malcolm would join the ranks of the unemployed. His job of transcription secretary became obsolete when computers replaced typewriters, and managers no longer dictated letters. Malcolm didn't accept the initial severance package the bank offered, and eventually received a more lucrative package.

During our phone conversations, Malcolm had told me about his job search. He denigrated the personnel staff who he said were sending him to companies knowing they wouldn't hire him. He was a proud man, and I suspected he'd turned down jobs he thought were beneath him. Mother had bequeathed him the house, so he didn't have a mortgage payment, but his taxi fares, pub tabs, and frequent meals out must have depleted his severance money, and any other benefits he received. I recalled the last conversation I'd had with Malcolm, looking for clues. He'd seemed a bit agitated, something about an argument with his best friend, who was also blind. Malcolm said something else during that phone call.

"You know, Pauline," he'd said. "I was told recently that you're colored. I never knew that. I remember I was a bit confused a few years ago when Sheila and Doris (our two sisters), were arguing, and Sheila said Doris should donate money to a colored organization because of all the horrible things she said and did to you."

I didn't know how to respond. I almost laughed. First of all, I wasn't sure why donating to a "colored" organization should be Doris' penance for torturing me. Secondly, why would my skin color be a topic of conversation after all these years? After I'd hung up the phone I thought about what Malcolm had said. I'd no idea whether he ever knew what color my skin was, or that the Old Man wasn't my father. Malcolm's judgment of me, whatever it happened to be—was based on how he and I had interacted, and what he knew about my behavior. What was it Martin Luther King, Jr. had said: "I look to a day when people will not be judged by the color of their skin, but by the content of their character."

I would have said something to Malcolm a long time ago if he were a racist, and had made ugly comments about black people—both for my sake and his. My announcing the color of my skin to Malcolm would have been as odd to me as telling him Sheila had only one arm—if he didn't know already. Why?

Malcolm coming home from work during our visit to England in 1985

A TANGLED WEB

Thank God for the weddings. With the deaths of Eileen and Malcolm, the year 2007 would have been totally depressing had it not been for the announcements by our daughter, Tina, and our son, Aaron. They'd both chosen to get married the same year. It would be Tina's second marriage—a garden wedding at her home in Sacramento on one of the most popular dates of the year, 07.07.07. Aaron was getting married for the first time—another garden wedding, this one at his future mother-in-law's home in the coastal town of Half-Moon Bay. The weddings were one month apart. Fortunately, all I had to do was show up.

Tina was planning a honeymoon vacation which included a visit to England and to County Mayo, in Ireland—my mother's birthplace. Tina's husband-to-be, Brian, was of Irish ancestry too—something my mother would have appreciated.

"Have you been on the Castlebar website?" Tina asked me one afternoon, several weeks before her wedding.

"I checked out the 'Find your Mayo Roots' link a couple of times," I said, "but couldn't find anything about your grandmother's family."

My multi-tasking daughter was tapping on the computer keyboard while we were talking. "Mother," she yelled into the hands-free phone. "You will not believe this. There's a Michael Behan on the website inquiring about a Mary Kate O'Toole, and a Harry Behan. I'll send you the website link."

I was speechless. Harry Behan was the name of the Old Man.

I opened the link that Tina sent, and read the following:

> "*Michael James Behan*
> *Seeking: Mary Kate O'Toole, Harry (Henry)Behan*
> *Details: I'm the son of John (Jackie)J. Behan,*
> *Born in Castlebar 19 Apr 1928. I'm just looking for*
> *family, friends and others that may have known*
> *John. He passed, regrettably, in March of this year."*

I was surprised and intrigued to see the names O'Toole, Behan, and the city of Castlebar linked together. How many Harry Behan's could there have been in Castlebar? Behan is not a common name—and who was this Kate O'Toole with the same last name as Uncle Jim, my mother's half-brother?

I dashed off an e-mail to Michael detailing what I thought was a family connection. The website posting was several years old, so I didn't expect to get a response. To my surprise I received a reply several days later.

> "Pauline,
>
> *Greetings from Virginia. It truly never ceases to amaze me how small the internet has made the world! I haven't checked my AOL e-mail in months until this morning (I use a different e-mail almost exclusively) and imagine my surprise. Unless there's some HUGE coincidence, the records you speak of must refer to my paternal grandmother and grandfather."*

Michael, I discovered through subsequent e-mails, was the *grandson* of Harry Behan—the Old Man. I was astonished. This meant the Old Man had fathered another child, Michael's father. I was to learn more shocking details.

The Old Man had been married before in Ireland. His first wife was Kate O'Toole, with whom he'd fathered not just one son—Michael's father, John Joseph in 1928—but two others: Noel (born in 1938), and Stephen (born in 1939). Michael, or Mick, as he signed off—using the Irish and British nickname—reported his father, John, and his Uncle Stephen had both passed away. Noel was still alive and living in Phoenix.

It appeared from the birthdates of the Irish sons, that when Harry immigrated to England with my mother, he left behind his wife, Kate, and young son John Joseph. The ten years between the first and second son suggested Harry had returned to his wife in the 1930's and fathered two more children before going back to England and settling down with my mother.

I thought the story couldn't get any more bizarre, but it did. I learned from Mick that the O'Toole surname was no coincidence. Kate O'Toole was my Uncle Jim's sister, and Mother's half-sister. What's more, it dawned on me that Catholic Ireland prohibited divorce until sometime in the 1990's. The Old Man and Mother could never have married. Oh, my God! Now it became clear why Mother and the Old Man never talked about their past—about their Irish families—and why there were no wedding photographs. There had been no wedding! Then, I'm almost ashamed to admit, a smile crossed my face. Apparently I wasn't the only little bastard in the family.

More information flowed from Michael. I learned the Old Man was as cruel to his Irish sons as he was to all of

"Fudge"

us. "My father related many stories of abuse as a child whenever Harry would come back to town. He was always out of work, and angry, and would come back to Castlebar just long enough get Mary Kate pregnant and use my father as a whipping post. My father joined the RAF in the '40's to get away from Castlebar and, while in England stayed many times with Tom (your uncle) and Anne Halligan."

All of the Irish sons eventually emigrated to the United States—first to Chicago in the 1950's and later to Phoenix, Arizona. My Uncle Tom, his wife Anne, and their three children John, Desmond, and Brenda would eventually join them in Arizona—emigrating from London in the early '70's. Uncle Tom had visited just once in Wellingborough, in the 1950s, by himself. I didn't know he had a wife, or any children.

Since I never knew my biological father, I treasured these snippets of history on my mother's side, and wanted to know more. For some time, I had wondered who was pictured in an old black and white photograph I found among my mother's belongings after she died. The snapshot pictured an elderly man and woman, a young man in his thirties, and three school-aged children. They were crouched in a field by a stone wall—a setting reminiscent of the Irish countryside. I scanned the photo and sent it to Michael.

An answer came back at almost warp speed, traveling the 2400 miles from Virginia to California in less than a few minutes. I was still amazed by the internet.

"I've seen a similar photo. That is your grandmother and grandfather. It's also Tom (my uncle), and his 3 children, John, Des, and Brenda."

I stared at the photograph for ages. These were my

mother's parents. The woman in the photograph was quite large, and the man was slightly built—like my mother and Uncle Tom.

I had little sense of any extended family beyond my mother's brothers, Jim and Tom, and the Old Man's brother Bill, and his wife and three daughters. Now, at least, I had a photograph of my grandparents—not so unusual in most families, but astonishing in mine.

More photographs flew across cyber space. I was never so eager to open an e-mail in my life. One e-mailed photograph in particular caused me to shake my head in disbelief—a group photograph that included Uncle Tom's three children—my first cousins—John, Desmond, and Brenda. It looked as if someone had super-imposed a picture of my eldest son, Dean, in the back row. There was a remarkable resemblance between Dean, and my cousin John. When I sent the photograph to Dean, even he wondered how he came to be in the picture.

Michael was curious about his grandfather, and asked for a photograph of the Old Man. I didn't have one, so I sent him a picture of my brother Kevan, who looked the most like the Old Man. Michael shot back an e-mail exclaiming disbelief. My brother, Kevan, he stated, was the absolute image of his Uncle Stephen, one of Harry's Irish sons. This shouldn't have been a total surprise since Stephen was Kevan's half-brother.

I asked Michael if his family had spoken about my mother. The only information he had was that Uncle Tom had a sister they called, "Lizzie." *So, my mother had three names to go with her three lives: Lizzie the Irish girl; Bette—the "wife" of the Old Man; and Liz—Sid's wife.*

What a tangled hereditary web the Old Man and my mother had woven. Because the Old Man was married to my mother's half-sister, Kate, he was both the father, and uncle by marriage, to the children he'd had with my mother. Although he wasn't my father, since he was married to my mother's half-sister—he was, in fact, my uncle. These curious interlocking relationships sounded a lot like the scratchy vinyl record we listened to as kids on "His Master's Voice" wind-up gramophone—which ended with, "I'm my own grandpa..."

    I shared what I had learned about my family with our three adult children. They were interested, but not nearly as astonished as I was. I think the generational distance softened the impact on them, and two of three were getting married, and understandably pre-occupied.

    Both weddings went off without a hitch. Well, actually there were two hitches. Tina's wedding day was predicted to be one of the hottest days of the year—triple digits. To everyone's relief the weather cooled down two days before the wedding. The wedding date was so popular that several of our daughter's guests arrived at a wedding down the street, and poured themselves drinks before they realized they were at the wrong house.

    Our son Aaron's wedding ceremony was held at Becky's home in an open meadow. All the guests were seated on benches constructed by our son over several frenetic weekends. As Becky floated down the hill towards her groom, her bridal veil snagged on a bush. Becky laughed and kept on going. I thought her reaction boded well for any future marital difficulties.

Aaron and Becky
August 2007

Tina and
Brian
July 2007

Two of the Old Man's three Irish sons: (L-R)Johnnie and Noel, and his grandson, Michael

Irish grandparents: John and Sarah Halligan with Uncle Tom and his three children—John, Desmond, and Brenda

Back row (L-R) Brenda, Lee, Trudie, Steven,
John & Desmond
Front (L-R) Jen, James, Christina & Suzanne Halligan
family 1986

(L) My son, Dean. Note the resemblance to John in the upper photograph.

A GOOD BUZZ

The rambling ranch-style house where Jim and I had lived for the past twenty years, was our fifth home—if you could count our first place, the sparse apartment in Sin City, as a home. When we first viewed the house we were impressed with the open floor plan, the high ceilings, and the quality of the construction. Jim had run his hands over the dark wood paneling in the family room—"It's tongue and groove," he'd said admiringly. "This is hand-laid with no glue or nails." A series of events allowed us to purchase that house which normally would have been beyond our financial reach.

Three weeks after first arriving in California from England I was lucky enough to find work. I was hired as a receptionist-bookkeeper by J.V. Equipment Company, a business that sold meat tenderizing equipment from a store-front office. I was the lone office support. The company was owned by two men, John and Vern, who lived in Burlingame in the San Francisco Bay Area. The Sacramento office was operated by Bob, the son of one owner, and Ron, the mechanic. Vern, the "V" in JV Equipment Company, travelled up from the Bay Area every couple of months. Before he left the office after each visit, he would peer over the counter at me and say, "Have you bought a place yet? Doesn't matter what it looks like – just buy it."

Jim and I were in no financial position to buy a house. I was driving a 20-year-old Chevy with a driver seat worn so low I could barely see out of the windshield. Neither of us was earning a lot. Jim had recently been accepted into a construction apprenticeship program, but was off work during winters. My job with the State of California was several years away.

In less than a year, we'd moved from the sparse apartment in Sin City, to a two-bedroom place, and then to a three-bedroom duplex where we lived when Vern was giving me the financial pep talks.

The duplex came up for sale. I wanted to buy it. Only posh people owned their homes where I grew up. I was impressed that so many people owned their own homes in America, and they didn't seem posh. I don't know whether it was status or security that motivated me, but I was determined to buy the duplex. Jim eventually agreed—prodded by an assertive female realtor who repeatedly told us, "I'll make it happen"—which she did.

News arrived a year later that the small house in Texas that my ex-husband and I had purchased, was in danger of being foreclosed. I had no idea we still owned it. There was no mention of the house in the divorce decree. Someone must have convinced Frank to sign a Quit Claim Deed transferring the house to me, since I refused to sign it over to him as he requested.

The sale of the Texas house netted us enough to buy a house with ten acres of land. The house looked like a shack from the outside, but was surprisingly modern inside—even had a laundry room. I would have purchased the house for this feature alone. My wash days had begun in laundromats, progressed to communal apartment facilities, then to the height of luxury—my own washing machine and dryer in the duplex garage.

"Fudge"

It was the land that we wanted, though. Tina was 12 years old and mad about horses. She'd been taking riding lessons for over a year, which convinced us that her love for horses wasn't just a passing fancy. With the help of Jim's Uncle Bob, an experienced horseshoer, we bought a gentle Appaloosa mix named Raven.

I'd watch Tina from the front window as she groomed her mare. She looked so small leaning against the large muscular animal as she bent to clean the hooves. Her friend Gwen would ride up and the two would canter off across our field then out into the surrounding countryside. I couldn't even dream of such a life when I was her age.

Jim and I could hardly be accused of being financial geniuses—that would have taken deliberate action, and most of our decisions were serendipitous.

In 1980, a couple of years after moving onto the ten acres, and about the time I became pregnant with my third child, and Jim's first. Our ten acres was re-zoned to accommodate multiple housing estates. Land speculating agents began lining up to purchase our property. Each offer exceeded the one before. Jim finally received an offer he couldn't refuse. I practically danced out of the real estate office with a substantial check clutched in my fingers. It was this money that allowed us to purchase the large Elk Grove house.

Shortly after we moved in, our real-estate agent, Bev Miller, dropped by one morning carrying a plant as a house-warming gift. As we sat in the dining area of the kitchen drinking coffee, I asked her who lived in the house next door—the one with the row of tall Cyprus trees that lined the long driveway.

"That's Max," she said. "He's a self-made millionaire. He once owned all of the property in this court. He split it into four parcels, and sold three of them."

"You know," she continued. "When you guys decided to buy, I was worried about Max."

I was confused.

"Worried?" I said.

"He's from Oklahoma," she whispered as if he could hear through the walls and over the half-acre of land that separated us. Without waiting for a response, Bev picked up her purse that could have doubled as a suitcase—and left.

Once again I didn't get it. Didn't understand that someone, any white person, could look at me and see someone different from them. I didn't see someone different when I looked at them. What's more, Max was from Oklahoma, for God's sake. I was English! I frequently forgot I was a naturalized American.

"Max is okay," Jim said nonchalantly when I told him that evening what Bev had said. "He flagged me down in the driveway tonight and invited us over for a drink tomorrow."

There would be many evenings when Jim and I would sit with Max and his elegant wife, Eunice, sipping wine poured from a box. Max prided himself on buying cheap wine. The four of us would loll on cushioned outdoor furniture under the sheltered front patio between the columns of what Jim and I referred to as "Max's mansion," looking out over an expansive manicured lawn that led down to his man-made pond. I'd seen the pond being excavated. Whenever there was work to be done on Max's property, a work crew of muscular Hispanic men would magically appear, work like the devil in the sweltering heat, and then disappear until the next job.

I rarely saw Max without a smile. He was not a tall man, but his booming voice and his swagger made him an imposing presence.

"Pauline, how the hell are you?" he'd yell whenever he saw me outside. More than once we'd bump into each other at the mailboxes at the end of our driveways.

"Picking up my Social Security check," the millionaire would shout gleefully, waving an envelope in the air.

Our young son, Aaron, and Max's grandson, Jesse, became good friends. Max was as indulgent and generous with Aaron as he was with his grandson. Aaron had the run of Max's place. He was free to zoom up and down the winding driveway on his Big Wheels, and scamper in and out of the mansion to play with the plethora of toys Max stored for Jesse's visits. One afternoon, after returning from an outing with Jesse and Max, Aaron ran into the house carrying a large box.

"What have you got?" I asked.

"Grandpa took me and Jesse to Toys-R-Us," Aaron answered with a big grin spreading across his sweet face.

"He told us we could pick out anything in the store that we wanted."

No mention was ever made by us, or Max, as to why, exactly, the realtor was worried when we first moved into the neighborhood.

The house in Elk Grove had seemed large when all the children were home, and felt cavernous after they left. Besides, Jim wanted to move to the foothills and spend his retirement years smelling Mountain Misery, and gazing up at emerald pines. Water had to be nearby, too.

Jim never wavered in his vision. I wasn't so sure about what I wanted. I knew what I didn't want. I didn't want to be isolated. Some of the areas we visited in our search for the perfect place felt like we had left California, and taken a right turn into the Appalachians.

On one excursion we drove for miles without seeing a soul, just a collection of silver-grey mailboxes riddled with bullet holes. Squinting through road rock dust clouds at paint-peeling signposts, I barely made out such scenic and inviting names as Robbers Ravine, Mosquito Road, Widows Peek, Coyote Creek, Coyote Hill, and just in case we didn't get it—Coyote Mountain. I was waiting for toothless mountain men, armed with shotguns, to leap into our path—accompanied by the sound of dueling banjos—a horrible stereotype seared into my memory by the 1972 film classic, *Deliverance*.

I wasn't too far off with the toothless image. In one single weekend trip, after taking one of our frequent wrong turns, we rumbled by a shirtless man mowing a lawn. This was hardly an unusual sight on a hot Saturday morning except the lawn was in the middle of nowhere, enclosed by a six-foot chain-link fence, and the avid gardener had a rifle slung over his shoulder. We drove further down the road looking for a less threatening citizen we could ask directions, and ended up interrupting another gardener weed eating with a goat tied to his waist.

Another weekend we set off to view a piece of property which, judging by the description in the newspaper was exactly what we were looking for. I was not impressed, and refused to get out of the car when we arrived. The property was too secluded—I couldn't see any signs of life. I wouldn't roll down my window despite the rising temperature inside the car. Jim found my fears amusing, as usual, and smiled as he got out of the car. I had to admit the acreage was picturesque, even from my limited vantage point—slunk down in the passenger seat.

"Roll down the window," Jim urged when he returned to the car. "It is so peaceful up here."

I did so, reluctantly, only to roll it back up again almost immediately when I heard the sound of gun shots. We couldn't see anyone. Jim jumped back into the car a lot faster than he'd stepped out.

"These people are nuts," I said, immediately assigning mental incompetence to everyone in the area. As we drove warily back down the gravel road we spotted the source of the gunfire. There was a shooting range not 500 yards from the property. There was nothing more to be said.

It would take weeks before I recovered sufficiently from one foothill adventure, to try another. When Jim coaxed me out again, he'd avoid the more desolate areas. He wasn't able to distract me, however, from the highway signs which increased my anxiety each vertical mile we travelled—signs warning: "Runaway Truck Ramp"—"Rock Slide Area"—Mud Slide Area" and "One-lane Bridge—Travel at Your Own Risk."

I was traumatized by events which hardly fazed Jim. "It could have happened anywhere," he said casually after a pack of six howling Rottweilers appeared from nowhere, and chased the car down the road before returning to goodness knows what, hidden amongst the trees. To be honest, I secretly loved most of the areas we visited. I could feel an involuntary smile as we slowly climbed the grade, and left the flat land and summer smog behind in the Valley. The snow-tipped mountains would gradually appear in the distance, and the scrub oaks would give way to a forest of Ponderosa pines. Once we left the highway, I never stopped being surprised at how quickly the landscape could change. Sturdy log cabins reminiscent of the Old West were interspersed with rambling ranch houses with manicured lawns, then shabby trailers surrounded by rusting pickup trucks.

"No CC & R's here," I'd sniff, referring to my husband's refusal to live in any neighborhood controlled by Covenants, Conditions, and Restrictions. He wanted to be able to park his old cars wherever he wanted.

Jim was on the lookout for property near water, and his interest was piqued with what started with a Monday morning call from Tom, one of his construction crew. Tom explained he wouldn't be at work that day because he was having truck problems. The vehicle in question was a utility truck fitted with a small crane and a compressor, and heavily used on the job site. Jim, the construction superintendent, called the company mechanic later to see how long the repairs would take. The shop mechanic sounded amused.

"The truck will be out of commission for a while," he said, "it rolled cab-first into a pond.

Tom had been helping a friend move out of a rental house the owners were selling. The crane on the back of the company truck was ideal for lifting his friend's Harley motorcycle onto his pickup truck. It was evening and Tom had put the company truck in reverse to activate the bright backup lights so they could see what they were doing. Once the motorcycle was in the pickup bed, Tom locked down the crane and helped his friend tie the bike down. Both men had their backs to the company truck. As they worked they noticed the light was getting dimmer. When they finally turned around, it was too late. The company truck had ever-so-slowly rolled down the slight incline into the pond adjacent to the house. The crane neck had acted as a counter balance when it was extended during the lift, but once it was cranked down, the weight shifted, and the rest was history.

As Jim told the story I sensed he was more interested in the pond than the fate of the company truck. He was,

"Fudge"

and lost no time questioning Tom about the pond property, and drove out to the location as soon as he could. Seeing no "For Sale" sign at the house he logged this in his mental list of places to track.

One Saturday morning, Jim suggested we venture out again to check a piece of property in Nevada City. He described it as a nice piece of land with a year-round stream. Jim knew I was still in recovery mode and needed a bribe to get me back out this soon. He promised me dinner at Friar Tuck's, one of our favorite restaurants. As we motored up Highway 80 in deep conversation, we missed the Highway 49 off-ramp to Nevada City.

"As long as we missed the turn, "Jim said, "let's take a side trip to some property on the Bear River (another cuddly name), and we'll have something to compare to the Nevada City property."

We took the off-ramp leading to the Bear River property. As we pulled up to a four-way stop, we saw a "For Sale by Owner" sign. Jim suggested we take a look. "This is the area where the truck went into the pond," he explained, "Wouldn't it be weird if this was the house?" It was.

Jim steered the car down the narrow driveway between the house and a row of pine trees on the hillside—their roots exposed from years of eroding soil. As we stepped out of the car, Jim and I looked at each other. The only sound was the soft rustle of the breeze in the trees. The property was a forest of pines, oaks, and fragrant cedars. The infamous pond lay still, separating the house from another on the opposite hillside. A small shimmering lake was just visible through a forest of pines to the West. I was pleasantly surprised to say the least.

A tall, attractive young woman, with long dark hair, greeted us at the door.

"I'm Joan," she said in a husky voice, as she extended her hand. Joan explained she and her two brothers had inherited the property.

"My mother died about a year ago," she said. "My brother, Bruce, and I decided to sell 'as is' since we couldn't agree on renovations after we moved the renters out."

She went on to say her father died some years ago. He'd been a merchant seaman and had built the house.

"He had to live near water," she said softly. I knew Jim would have liked him.

Joan gave us a tour of the house. It was a two-story, with the living quarters on the upper level where we entered. The ground floor ran the length of the upper level, and was unfinished, except for a garage. Jim spent some time talking to Joan about such things as wells, sewers, and water rights. I tuned them out as I looked apprehensively at the outdated blue shag carpet, brown and orange floor tiles, dilapidated kitchen cabinets, and the unsightly, hanging, plucked chicken design on the tiles above the broken-down stove.

This would need a lot of renovation.

We left Joan with a promise to call her with a decision. As we journeyed on to our original Nevada City destination, I did something uncharacteristic. I asked Jim if he wanted to stop for a beer in Colfax, the next small town. Surprised, but pleased I seemed to be relaxing, Jim immediately pulled into the closest pizza parlor. "We don't want to order any food," Jim told the man behind the counter who had his pen poised. "Just two beers." A smile spread across the face of the pizza man. "I understand," he said knowingly, "you don't want to spoil a good buzz with food."

When he turned his back I looked at Jim and rolled

my eyes. As the pizza man reached into the cooler for the beer, a woman came up to the counter and asked if they served tomato beer.

"No," he said pleasantly, "but I can plop in some pizza sauce."

"That'll work," she said.

Jim and I smiled at each other. As we sat down by the window to drink our cold beer, I asked Jim if he had his tape measure with him. "Let's get some measurements," I suggested.

Jim told me later, "When you asked about the tape measure, I knew this was it."

Returning to the house from the opposite direction we passed a sign we hadn't seen before. It said Eden Valley. We had found our perfect place.

I could have used a crystal ball back in those early cold, damp, chaotic days at 84 Mannock Road in Wellingborough. What a difference it would have made to know this is where I would end up—soaking up the California sun—greeted each morning by the smell of pine and cedar trees, the quacking of ducks, the honking of Canada Geese, and the sight of baby deer bounding over the dam.

I would've known I'd eventually be nurtured by a caring husband, loved by my family, and valued by friends.

The view from the deck of our perfect place

CONCLUSION

The Search

There'd been times when I'd look at photographs of World War II black G.I.'s, and search for a face I resembled. After my youngest son, Aaron, went through puberty and his straight brown hair turned black and curled, I imagined he looked like my father. When I'd come across a group photograph of World War II soldiers, during one of my sporadic internet searches, I'd look for someone who resembled Aaron.

It was during one of these searches that I stumbled across the name of a conference held in London at Carnegie House in Piccadilly on December 19, 1944. The name of the conference said it all: "Report of Conference on the Position of the Illegitimate Child Whose Father is Alleged to be a Coloured American." I was three months old in December 1944, and blissfully unaware that the conference was about me.

I was one of a handful or so of biracial kids in Wellingborough, a small market town in the East Midlands, about an hour and half by train from London. All of us were conceived during the Second World War—fathered by black American soldiers who would return to America, either not knowing, or not caring, that they had left their children behind.

Our town was small enough we knew of each other. As presented in my memoir, there was my best friend, Dawn, who lived up the street. There were also Mary, Josie, Anne, Christine and Geoff, and some others whom I saw, but never knew. I was an adult before I learned there were more than a thousand other children fathered by black Americans, scattered in other parts of Great Britain. I was more surprised to learn that twenty thousand babies were fathered by white G.I.'s.

Springing into action, with a speed not typically associated with government, forty welfare and religious agencies assembled in Carnegie House. The British Government realized that thousands of illegitimate children, abandoned by their American military fathers, could become a huge financial problem. Someone had to support these kids. Since the conference included the words, "... whose father is alleged to be a coloured American,"—there was a realization that, in addition to the stigma of illegitimacy, biracial children, and their mothers, could be discriminated against.

I have to say, that since about 130,000 black G.I's were stationed in Great Britain during the war years, and with few other men of color to suspect, the "alleged" part made me laugh.

The conference transcripts recorded the anecdotal stories by people with important titles who described the negative impact the large numbers of illegitimate children were having "on the fabric of British society." Married women, who were giving birth to most of these children, were seen as the greatest challenge. British soldiers, returning from a year or more overseas, were not exactly ecstatic to find their wives with an extra baby in the pram, especially a brown one. White babies were less conspicuous, and many were incorporated into the family

"Fudge"

without too much attention, if the husbands were forgiving. Keeping a brown baby in the home, however, would broadcast their wives had offered the black American visitors quite a bit more than tea and crumpets. Some attendees suggested shipping the babies off to America to be adopted by black families. The idea was nixed when others pointed out The Adoption Act forbade sending a child out of the country for adoption. I thought Miss Steel, General Secretary of the Church of England Welfare Council, deserved a retroactive hug when she responded that such an adoption would "be terribly cruel... it would add to their sense of being unwanted, not only that their mothers had given them up, but the country where they were born had given them up, too."

As much as I admired Miss Steel's humanity, there were times when I was made so miserable by the constant bombardment of racial slurs I'd have gladly opted to make a break for America.

The majority of those at the conference agreed that unmarried mothers should be encouraged to keep their babies and be provided financial support. This government assistance was predicted to continue for a while since an unmarried mother wasn't likely to be inundated with marriage proposals.

Placing these babies in special government Children's Homes, which were springing up around the country, was another solution which surfaced at the conference. It was noted that Learie Constantine, a West Indian celebrity cricket player, was raising money for one such Home in Wakefield, Yorkshire. When word got out, the League of Coloured Peoples was quick to point out to Constantine the Home should be open to all—"there had never been any segregation in England like that of the American Southern States, and South Africa."

Not all was doom and gloom. One attendee reported, "That many girls are proud of their babies and rather welcome a delightful coloured baby in the family." I found it heartening to read the majority of black soldiers were willing to accept paternity, and anxious to marry their girlfriends. I couldn't find evidence of any military regulations banning mixed marriages, but almost half the American states had criminalized interracial marriage, which must have been a big deterrent.

I realized, all these years later, how simple it would have been for my mother to have dumped me into one of those government Children's Homes—hiding me away—but she chose instead to keep me, and I honestly don't think it was for the few shillings a week she received in child allowance.

For years I'd struggled with asking my mother for the name of the man who'd fathered me. I was afraid of how she'd respond. I'd thought she'd be angry with me for bringing up something from the past—asking questions she didn't want to answer. I was also afraid for myself. What if she didn't know my father's name? How would I feel? If she did know his name and I traced him—what if he were a criminal? Would he still be alive? I told myself, some things are better left alone. But I couldn't leave it alone.

I didn't have the nerve to ask Mother for my father's name face-to-face during one of my trips back to England—nor even to ask over the phone. I wrote a letter. At that time I was in my forties, married with three children, and living in California.

The flimsy airmail envelope sat unopened on my kitchen table until I could stand it no longer.

"I don't remember his name," Mother wrote.

I wasn't surprised, but I was disappointed. Without

even a name, there was no hope of ever locating my father—a fantasy I'd entertained for as long as I could remember.

Over the years I'd heard that other biracial children in my hometown had searched for their fathers—with varying degrees of success. In the late '60s, when I'd returned to England while my first husband was in Vietnam, I'd read in our local paper, *The Evening Telegraph*, that one girl's American father returned to Wellingborough to meet her. Later she'd visit him in the United States. Another girl traced her father, only to discover he'd died a few years earlier.

Similar experiences were recounted by Janet Baker in her Master's dissertation, "Lest we Forget—The Children They Left Behind," published in 2000. Ms. Baker, herself a child of a black-American serviceman, and a British mother, had journeyed back to England from her adopted Australia, to interview eleven adult children of the same mixed race.

My eyes filled with tears as I read the interviewees' responses to Ms. Baker's questions. Their experiences were my experiences. We'd all suffered racial taunts, and had nobody to turn to for comfort, or empathy. How could our white mothers and siblings understand the depth of our pain, and our confusion for being singled out for abuse?

Several of the study participants had searched for their American fathers for years. Six of the eleven had found their fathers, three of whom were alive, and three had died. "The three respondents whose fathers were still alive had visited them in the United States. One father had also been to England on several occasions to spend time with his daughter."

Ms. Baker had used the term, "war babes," in her writing, and during my on-going research, I learned there was an organization with that name. Shirley McGlade was the leader of "War Babes," a group of 300 sons and daughters of American fathers, which was founded in Birmingham, England, in the 1980s. Collectively, they hoped to get information about their fathers from the U.S. National Personnel Records Center—the agency charged with storing the military personnel records of discharged and deceased veterans. The "War Babes," had difficulty getting requested information from the Personnel Center. They were told The Privacy Act of 1974, prevented the agency from releasing personal information about veterans.

The group, with the support of the Public Citizen Litigation Group in America, sued the Defense Department. The two-year legal battle ended with a settlement on November 16, 1990. The National Personnel Records Center, when provided with specific information, was required to provide members of War Babes the kinds of information they'd requested. I would hear about the Records Center again.

Unlike American correspondence, letters from England showed no return address, but I recognized the neat handwriting of my friend Dawn. When I opened the envelope, and unfolded the two lined pages, out slipped a black and white photograph of a soldier.

> *"Dear Pauline, It was lovely to hear from you I hope everyone is keeping well. Last year I did get in touch to try and find my father, but came up trumps. His name was William Chapman and he came from Texas that's all I can remember..."*

Dawn knew her father's name? She even had a photograph of him. I was astounded, and envious.

I'd learn that William Chapman and Dawn's mother kept in touch after he was shipped from England to Europe. He knew Dawn's mother was pregnant, and expected to return to England, but was sent home to the U.S. after the war ended. A black couple, who were friends with William, offered to adopt Dawn and take her to America. Dawn's mother refused to give her up.

I stared at the photograph of Dawn's father. He was wearing a military jacket, and a helmet. His pencil-thin moustache arched from his upper lip to just under his nose. As I studied the photograph, I could see a resemblance between the soldier and my friend, except for the eyes. The soldier's eyes looked sorrowful. Dawn's eyes twinkled. She looked as if she were holding in a burst of giggles, which often prompted an attack of them from me. I continued to scrutinize the photograph, asking myself if I looked like him. Did my son, Aaron, look like him? Could Dawn be the sister I always wanted her to be? I couldn't see the resemblance I craved.

It was news to me that Dawn had been trying for several years to locate her father. In subsequent correspondence she provided additional information. She'd contacted the U.S. National Personnel Records Center—the agency the War Babes had taken to court. The Center informed her they needed additional information in order to trace her father. They needed more from Dawn than just her father's name. Dawn didn't own a computer and hoped, since I did have one, and was living in America, it might be easier for me to find the information she needed.

I was excited. All hope of finding my father had evaporated, but I could at least have the satisfaction of helping my friend find hers.

Although I had a name, a photograph, and a few other details about Dawn's father, I didn't have some of the most important information such as his service or social security number, or his military unit. I studied the photograph of William Chapman with a magnifying glass, looking for clues.

On the top front of the soldier's helmet was a broad painted white arc. Underneath were two painted chevrons over the letter tee. A quick Internet search of World War II army ranks revealed the two chevrons and the "T" represented the rank of Technician Fifth Grade. That meant he wasn't a Private—someone who'd just been conscripted.

Dawn had written that her father was stationed in our hometown, and in Kettering, a town about eight miles north of Wellingborough. The white G.I.'s had barracks at Chelveston Airbase, the closest U.S. base to our town, and the black G.I.'s were billeted in town—somewhere. This pattern of racial segregation was repeated throughout Great Britain—white G.I.'s stationed at official airbases, while black G.I.'s were billeted off base, at obscure sites. It would be three years after the war, in 1948, before President Harry Truman would desegregate the military.

I e-mailed the *Northamptonshire Telegraph*, the successor of *The Evening Telegraph*, hoping their archives included articles about black G.I.'s, which could identify their units. I was told the archives going back to World War II had not been digitized. In fact, digital files had only been available since 2005. I should have known.

On one of my trips to Wellingborough, I'd visited the town library on Pebble Lane, where the pawn shop used to be. At the time I wasn't looking for information about black G.I.'s, but searching for a photograph of my stepfather, the Old Man. I knew nobody in our family had a photograph of him, and although he wasn't exactly beloved, I thought my children and grandchildren might like to see what he looked like. As a child, I remembered seeing a photograph of the Old Man in *The Evening Telegraph*, with a huge snake around his neck. I had a vague idea of the year, but couldn't recollect any other details. I was dismayed to discover microfilm—a labor-intensive process—was the only method available for archival retrieval. I spent hours in the library searching for this photograph, but without specific dates, the search appeared endless. I gave up.

I did find one on-line article about American soldiers in Wellingborough. The *Northamptonshire Telegraph* published a piece aptly titled, "Rooting out Details on Black Soldiers" by Mike Parnell, a project organizer of a community group in Wellingborough. The group, I read, is dedicated to uncovering details about the American military artifacts discovered during restoration of The Victoria Centre, on Palk Road. Mr. Parnell contacted the US Army Heritage Center for more information, and was told that 30 black G.I.'s were billeted in the building in August 1942, but offered no additional details.

I telephoned the US Center, hoping to identify the American unit that was stationed at the Wellingborough Centre, and was promised a return call.

I never received that call.

William Chapman – Dawn's father

THE REST OF THE STORY
Summer 2019

Unlike me, my biracial English friend, Dawn had known the name of her African-American father. She also knew that he came from Texas. Best of all, she possessed a photograph of him.

Dawn had contacted the U.S. National Personnel Records Center hoping to locate her father, or at the very least, a member of his family. The Center requested more information. Did she have a military service number, or a Social Security number? Dawn had neither. She wrote and asked me for help. I was living in America and had a computer—two things she thought would guarantee success.

Armed with a name, a photograph, access to a computer and living in the country where her father was born, I was no more successful at locating Dawn's father.

How then could I, with no name and no photograph, ever hope to locate my own father?

I stopped looking.

Years later, in 2006, my daughter, Tina, and I succumbed to a sales promotion from ancestry.com and submitted our DNA. Our trust in the process was confirmed when the match came back:

Possible range: Parent, Child – immediate family member. Confidence: Extremely High.

We laughed.

For the next 13 years I would receive evidence of DNA matches on my Irish mother's side—interesting, but not what I was seeking. Matches on the African-American side were third, fourth, fifth cousins that lead nowhere. In May 2019, I received notice of another match on the African-American side:

Possible range: 1st – 2nd cousins. Confidence: Extremely High.

A first or second cousin! I contacted the match immediately:

Dear Nellie: Ancestry shows that you and I may be 1st or 2nd cousins. I was born in England ...

I provided Nellie with additional information about my background. I cited my memoir so she could read more about me, and know I'd been searching for my father for decades. A response came back:

Pauline: I read the excerpts from your book and was thoroughly impressed with your courage. Although you had a challenging beginning, you have overcome and thrived. Thank God!

Very kind words, I thought. The email continued...

My mother's brother that was in the service, was too young to be your father.

Oh no. Another dead end. I read on...

My father and his brothers all served in the military.

My heart thumped. They were in the military. My hopes rose...

Unfortunately, they have all passed away.

Here we go again...

Based on your information, I have eliminated all but one brother.

All but one? That meant one possibility remained. I pulled myself together and read the final sentence:

However, I would like to share this information with my cousins before giving you his name. Please give me a few days to discuss this with them. Nellie

I rate myself high on the "stiff upper lip" scale and yet, when I read the email to my husband, I burst into tears. My husband looked apprehensive. He was concerned, he told me later, that nothing would come of this. He knew how long I'd been searching.

I allowed myself to get excited. A first cousin meant that the cousins Nellie was asking for permission could possibly be my half-siblings.

But what if the cousins have a different opinion of me than Nellie? They may not want to connect with me, or to share their father's name. From my memoir Nellie knew my age and my current circumstances. It would be obvious that I wasn't looking for material gain.

That may not matter, though. I'd read Lucy Bland's sensitive and compassionate book, *Britain's 'Brown Babies,'* that chronicled the lives of more than 40 mixed-race British children—like me, the offspring of Caucasian mothers and African-American fathers. In her chapter: *Secrets and Lies: Searching for mothers and fathers*, several of Professor Bland's interviewees revealed that not all their father's American families welcomed them with open arms.

I re-read Nellie's email. *She writes well. And the fact that she wouldn't share more information without consulting her cousins showed she was a considerate person, respectful of her cousins' privacy.*

I liked this family already.

For several days, first thing each morning I stumbled to my computer housed in a small tan armoire at the far end of my dining room. Light floods in through the window on my right. Normally I spend time gazing at the Mule Deer as they move cautiously up a narrow path and into the pine trees. Those mornings, a herd of elephants could have trooped by me and I wouldn't have seen them. I found myself glued to the computer monitor hoping for the email from Nellie.

Several days later it came.

> *Pauline:*
>
> *I can only imagine how anxious you must be awaiting an answer to this vital missing piece of your life. My cousin, Carol, and I spoke this evening and she has given me permission to release her father's name to you. His name was Leroy Coker; he served in the Army until 1945.*

Leroy Coker. I finally knew the name of my father. The air around me went still. I whispered the name several times. Nellie continued...

> *He, like your mother, is also deceased. I also have a picture of him when he was in the Army, but this Ancestry message center does not allow me to include any attachments or paste a picture. I will email it to you via my email address.*

A picture! Not only did I now know my father's name, I would soon see his face. I was glad there was no one in the house who could see my face. I must have looked shell-shocked. The rest of the email offered more good news.

> *Not only did Carol agree to release his name, she also*

"Fudge"

said that you could correspond with her via her email address. I am glad that you were able to find this missing piece to your ancestry and pray that it gives you peace. Blessings to you, Nellie

I loved them both.

The forwarded email from Nellie's personal account had a subject line that read: Picture of Leroy Coker. As luck would have it, Carol had been collecting photographs for the family reunion and forwarded the photograph of her father to Nellie.

I opened the attachment and downloaded the photograph. The first image I saw was a boot and the loop of a shoelace. Next came a trouser leg with a smart crease. The photograph was downloading upside down! Then the entire email disappeared. Was I dreaming? Then the image reappeared and slowly finished downloading. I'm too old to stand on my head. I printed the attachment.

I spent most of the day staring at the face on the photograph through a magnifying glass. Thank goodness he was nice looking, I thought, then chastised myself for being so shallow. Did I have his eyes? His eyebrows? What about the nose? This was a formal pose. He was sitting in a chair, one leg crossed, supported by the knee of the other leg. He was wearing a military uniform. Was this how he looked when he and my mother met and had what I politely refer to as "a liaison?"

When I emerged from my stupor, I responded to Nellie and Carol:

> Dear Nellie and Carol: I cannot tell you what it means to have a name, and especially to see the face of my father. It is overwhelming! ... Thank you so much. The photograph is especially precious be-

cause Leroy is in uniform and may be at the age that my mother met him.... I am so looking forward to connecting with your family to the extent that it's comfortable for you.

Over the next few weeks emails flew back and forth, followed by phone conversations. I learned most of the family lived in Pittsburgh, Pennsylvania. Members of this new American family were obviously surprised to learn they had an additional relative, one born in England no less.

Then came the first email from Carol:

Hello Pauline (My Sister),

My sister! What a sweet way to start her letter. She's already claiming me as her sister.

I am full of excitement, curiosity and joy. My (our) Cousin Nellie provided me with some background information and I do have lots of questions, however, unsure of where to begin.

Leroy is my father and I am one of nine children born to him and my mother. Two brothers and one sister have departed this earthly home. Also, we have another older brother by another mother born prior to dad entering the military. He would be considered the eldest child. He was introduced to the family during my late teens. Our father's two youngest sisters (in their 80's) might be able to share some of dad's military and other history with me.

There are also four other siblings from my mom's first marriage. We are all sisters and brothers. Now, I have 14 siblings instead of 13!!!!!

I plan to share this new found information with my siblings this coming weekend. Hopefully, they will be just as excited and eager to know more. It would be great to connect with your daughter (my niece). I do not have any social media accounts so we will communicate via email and phone. I hope this is alright with you.

If you are available, I would like to call you this evening after my last meeting of the day. This will be around 8:30 my time and 5:30 in California. God Bless, Carol

My response:

Hello Carol:

Should I also add, "my sister" I thought? But I'm emotionally repressed, and knew it would take me time to write those words. How I envy people like Nellie and Carol, and my daughter, Tina, who can easily embrace someone and share their feelings. My email continued...

Excitement indeed! My goodness. I am also one of nine children—only not one of them looked like me! Now I have a whole new family. I am so looking forward to hearing from you. How wonderful that two of your aunts are still alive and may be able to provide more history.

As soon as I received the first email from Nellie naming my father I'd shared it with my three children. My two sons were interested, but it was my daughter, Tina, who'd begun this genetic journey with me, who was the most excited.

I'd shared all the Pittsburgh emails with her and she

was communicating individually with several relatives. I received a copy of a response from Carol to one of Tina's emails.

> Tina:
>
> I appreciate your sharing this lovely and vivid picture of your mom. It provides such an image of a warm and caring individual. It is my prayer that this is only the beginning of a wonderful connection with my extended family. I believe this is going to be an exciting journey as we forge ahead in sharing about our family experiences—past and present.

Via subsequent phone conservations I discovered a Coker family reunion had been planned for July 27, just a couple of months away. Tina, who is always up for an adventure, declared, "We have to go!"

And we did.

Late in the evening of July 25, 2019, Tina and I were met at the Pittsburgh Airport by Cousin Nellie and her daughter, Marcy. Their beautiful faces, ones we recognized from Facebook, were wreathed in smiles. Bodies were hugged and joyful greetings exchanged. Tina and I were being welcomed so warmly by two people, who only a few months earlier didn't know we existed.

Off we sped in Marcy's car to the Cambria Hotel.

We exchanged gifts on the way. California-themed items, including our favorite Blue Diamond chocolate covered almonds, were handed forward to Nellie from the backseat. Tina and I unfolded our gifts: black and gold T-shirts emblazoned with Pittsburgh baseball, "Let's Go Bucs," and the face of a ferocious buccaneer. This was the first hint that we were entering a sports-mad city.

Our hotel was next to the arena of the Pittsburgh

Penguins, the city's ice hockey team. Two days later, when Tina and I hopped on the hop-on-hop-off tour bus, we were awed by the giant stadium housing the city's most famous sports franchise, The Pittsburgh Steelers.

My outdated image of Pittsburgh was one of an industrial steel town, which of course it once was. Clear blue skies greeted us the morning we stepped outside our hotel, the result of the city's shift to cleaner industries.

Clear skies were not the only surprise. Who knew there are more than 400 bridges in the city, and not one, or two, but three rivers? The Allegheny and Monongahela Rivers converge to form the Ohio which flows down to the Mississippi. I learned this, and more, on a leisurely boat cruise the last evening of our trip. The river cruise was a gift to Tina and me from Carol and her engaging daughter, Arlisa, with whom Tina immediately bonded.

Now that I knew my father's name I was able to trace a 1940s census that revealed he was born in South Carolina. I imagined his family were among the 6 million African Americans that left the rural south to escape racial violence and find work in industrial northern cities such as Pittsburgh. This massive relocation, I'd learn later, was known as The Great Migration, an historical event I had not heard of, nor I'm ashamed to admit, would have held much interest. My world had been a white one, European centered.

Carol had arranged a 'meet and greet' at her house on Friday evening, the day after our arrival. She'd invited a few close relatives, an intimate gathering before meeting more than 150 or so family members expected at the reunion the following day.

Friday evening Tina pulled the rental car to the curb outside the address that Carol had texted that morning. A woman stood on the top step of the path to the house. As

I climbed the steps and grew closer I could see she was quite beautiful, but looked too young to be sister Carol. But it was Carol. She first threw her arms around me, and then Tina, and led us into her home. I was too overwhelmed to cry.

Inside people were milling around, and others dropped in throughout the evening. Carol introduced us as people came and went. I forgot their names immediately, and hoped I didn't look as dazed as I felt.

My daughter, who is more outgoing than I am, looked at home immediately, chatting with everyone. As I sunk down on a soft white sofa, someone handed me a family album. I slowly turned the pages making an effort to connect the faces in the photographs with the people in the room. This was an impossible task since many of the photographs were taken years before. I was mostly interested in seeing photographs of my father, and dwelled on one that was taken in his later years. I would see this photograph posted on a wall at the family reunion. Boisterous laughter and animated conversations filled the room throughout the evening. Many of those present had not seen each other for 16 years when the last family reunion was held in 2003.

All told I met six siblings—two sisters and four brothers. There was Carol, who hosted the meet-and-greet, and Nancy, the youngest sister. I'd meet Nancy's husband, Bobby, at the reunion. The four brothers were Leroy Jr., Charles, who drove down from New York in a spiffy red Maserati, Leonard and Danny. I also met lovely Anna, Leroy's wife. Sitting in a chair across from me was Antoinette, a niece affectionately known as Bunny. Her mischievous smile reminded me of my biracial girlhood friend, Dawn. One young man stood out, both because of his height and his good looks. He sat down next to me and chatted amiably. His name was Cleveland, the son of cousin Linda and her husband, Mack. He told me he'd graduated, but looked so young I assumed he was referring to high school. He repeated himself several times that it was college. Tina overheard the conversation and gave me the, "It's-time-to-go look."

Several weeks after I returned to California I received a phone call from another sister: Mattie. I'd met her son, Michael at Carol's house. He'd explained his mother's absence. She'd recently been discharged from the hospital. Mattie reiterated that on the telephone and we promised to stay in touch. I thought it was a lovely gesture that even though she was still recovering from a serious medical condition she took time to contact me.

My father Leroy had come from an unbelievably large family. His parents had 21 children, which included a couple of sets of twins. Leroy fathered 10 children, not including me.

Around 1p.m. the afternoon after the meet-and-greet, wearing our bright blue and green T-shirts embroidered with "We Are Family – Coker Family Reunion," a gift from Carol, we sped off to the reunion. Guided by Tina's Australian accented Siri, unintelligible to me, we arrived at the Pittsburgh's beautiful 250-acre Riverview Park. After unintentionally circling the area a few times, we mistakenly parked in the loading zone, and would eventually be blocked by vehicles that had a legitimate reason for parking there.

The picnic space was a cavernous covered area, walled on several sides, making it usable in all weather conditions. That day the weather couldn't have been more perfect—sunshine and no wind. Row upon row of picnic tables stood in two sections separated by a wide aisle where later in the day I would make a fool of myself trying to do the popular line dance, the Electric Slide.

When we entered I realized, once again, what a great idea Carol's 'meet and greet' was. I felt myself relax when I recognized those we'd met the evening before. I would have felt a lot more tense walking into a huge area full of people we were related to, but had never met. Seated across from me at the picnic table were Nellie and her grandson, Aiden. Nellie proudly proclaimed Aiden had garnered first prizes competing at each event during his educational summer camp.

Aiden is biracial. His mother is Marcy, Nellie's daughter, and his father is Kristian, who has Italian heritage. It was Kristian's exploration of his Italian heritage through Ancestry.com that sparked Nellie's interest. Intrigued by Kristian's DNA results, and inquisitive about her Native American heritage, Nellie purchased a DNA kit for $59.99 during a sales promotion, just as Tina and I did. I'd learn that Nellie rarely buys anything that isn't on sale or doesn't redeem a coupon.

Nellie ordered her DNA in August 2018. Her results came back a month later. These results did not show a match with either me or my daughter. It was only after Ancestry updated their testing procedures in 2019, that Nellie and I both received our updated Ancestry results, matching us as first or second cousins. Nellie's additional family research identified her Uncle Leroy as my father.

At the reunion I chose to sit at a picnic table where I could enjoy watching people as they walked through the large open entrance. I continued to be stunned that everyone I saw was a relative, and some looked like me. I grew up knowing only two uncles, one aunt, and three girl cousins—none of whom looked like me.

As I watched the entrance, an elderly woman entered, walking slowly as she leaned on a cane. White hair, styled in a smooth chin-length bob, framed her unlined face. Children rushed towards her. Aunt Shermell had arrived.

Knowing my father was born in 1919, I had assumed none of his siblings would be alive, and was thrilled to learn from Carol that two sisters, Shermell and Ivory, were alive and well and in their eighties.

I managed to awkwardly traverse the picnic bench without falling over, and stood waiting to greet Aunt Shermell when the welcoming group thinned.

"Don't be shy," Tina said, encouraging me to approach Shermell. I walked over and introduced myself. Aunt Shermell had not been at the Friday evening event, but I had spoken with her on the phone from California. We embraced, and I walked with her to a nearby bench. We sat and held hands. What do you say to the person who is one of the two oldest living relatives of a father you had searched for emotionally ever since you could remember? I honestly can't recall what either of us said. I do remember my feelings. Her words made me feel warm and wanted.

Aunt Ivory arrived a little later. She is small and slim with long dark hair—in her early eighties, a few years younger than Shermell. We sat and talked. I remember snippets of that conversation. Ivory said her brother, Leroy, had talked about his stay in England—how desperate for food many of the British were in their war-torn country. And how many of the G.I's had gladly shared their rations, some trading them for...she left words unsaid.

"Your mother kept you," she said squeezing my hand her eyes filling with tears. "And," she said, bringing me to tears, "My brother would have kept you too had he known."

Father: Leroy Coker – 1942 – Age 23

(L-R)Aunt Ivory and Aunt Shermell Coker Family Reunion Pittsburgh, PA 2019

Coker sisters (L-R) Back Row: Nancy and Annie
Front Row: Carol, Tina, Faye

Brothers and Nephews

(L-R) Front Row-Little Jerry and Jarome
Middle Row: Danny, Larry, Leonard, Edwin, Mike
Back Row: 2nd from left: Bill, Bob, Charles, Dwayne
(not pictured: Jerry, A.C., Tony)

Brother Leroy Jr. and me. Family Reunion 2019

(L-R) Cousin Nellie, my daughter Tina, Nellie's daughter, Marcy, and me. Greeting at Pittsburgh Airport 2019

Leroy Jr's wife, Sister-in-law, Anna

Cousin Marcy, her husband Kristian and their son Aiden-Pittsburgh 2019

ABOUT THE AUTHOR

The bucolic foothills of Northern California have been Pauline's home since she retired, and is where she lives with Jim, her husband of more than four decades.

Pauline spends her time writing, volunteering, and enjoying the antics of the local wildlife.

ALSO BY THE AUTHOR

Bonkers for Conkers

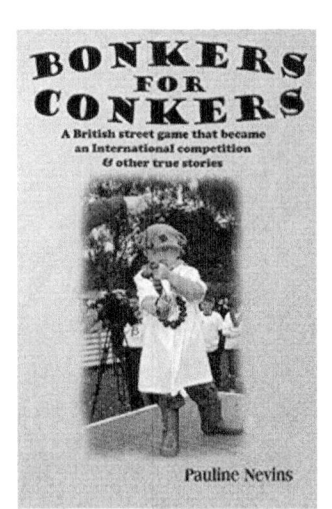

This collection of true stories, published as columns in the newspapers, *The Auburn Journal, and The Union,* delights the reader with tales of Pauline's unconventional Irish mother, her working-class British hometown, her reluctant European travels and her life in California's bucolic foothills.

*5.0 out of 5 stars on Amazon:
Funny and Heartfelt Short Stories*

Another book by Pauline that I loved. The short stories of her life in England and beyond had me laughing as I read through some of her experiences. There were other times when I felt anger at the inability of some people to understand how their actions can hurt others. Any time an author is able to engage the reader to this extent, they are successful, in my book! ...Another engaging read!

Kathy Norrell

Printed in Great Britain
by Amazon